D0843382

THE SPIRITUALITY OF
ST. TERESA OF AVILA

The Spirituality
of
St. Teresa
of Avila

Sr. Mary Alphonsetta
Haneman, C.S.S.F.

ST. PAUL EDITIONS

NIHIL OBSTAT:
  Rev. Richard V. Lawlor, S.J.
  Censor

IMPRIMATUR:
  ✠ Humberto Cardinal Medeiros
  Archbishop of Boston

Grateful acknowledgment is made for permission to quote from the following sources:

The Collected Works of St. Teresa of Avila, Volume I copyright © 1976, Volume II copyright © 1980, translated by Kieran Kavanaugh and Otilio Rodriguez. ICS Publications, 2131 Lincoln Road, N.E. Washington, D.C. 20002.

The Collected Works of St. John of the Cross. Translated by Kieran Kavanaugh and Otilio Rodriguez copyright © 1973 by Washington Province of Discalced Carmelites, Inc., ICS Publications, 2131 Lincoln Rd. N.E. Washington, D.C. 20002.

The Complete Works of St. Teresa of Jesus 3 vols., translated and edited by E. Allison Peers from the critical edition of P. Silverio de Santa Teresa, C.D. (New York: Sheed and Ward, Inc., 1946). Reprinted with permission of Andrews and McMeel, Inc., Fairway, Kansas, 66205.

Scripture texts used in this work are taken from the *New American Bible,* copyright © 1970, by the Confraternity of Christian Doctrine, Washington, D.C., and are used by permission of copyright owner. All rights reserved.

ISBN 0-8198-6843-4 cloth
     0-8198-6844-2 paper

Printed in the U.S.A. by the Daughters of St. Paul
50 St. Paul's Ave., Boston, MA 02130

The Daughters of St. Paul are an international congregation of religious women serving the Church with the communications media.

To my brothers, Henry and Chester,
my sister-in-law, Rose,
and the new generation.

Contents

Acknowledgments

The spiritual enrichment that accrued from my exposure to the writings of St. Teresa of Avila and St. John of the Cross was further augmented by the rich exchange of ideas and comments of extremely capable persons who worked with me in this undertaking. I would like to take this opportunity to express my gratitude to them all: to Rev. Walter Brennan, O.S.M., my thesis director, for his scholarly assistance and encouragement; to Rev. Hugo Amico and Rev. Patrick O'Brien, C.M., members of the thesis committee; to Rev. William Healy, O.C.D., whose Carmelite insight was a great help in editing the manuscript and whose spiritual conferences were a constant inspiration; to Rev. Matthew Baran, O.F.M., Conv., for his advice; to the Discalced Carmelite Community of Peterborough, N.H., for providing the "Desert" experience and for sharing their manuscripts; to my friends for their invaluable support; and to my Community, the Congregation of the Sisters of St. Felix of Cantalice, for giving me the opportunity to pursue my life-long goal of theological study.

In addition I would like to thank Rev. Robert Henle, S.J., former president of Georgetown University; Rev. James McCurry, O.F.M., Conv., and the members of the Secular Order of Discalced Carmelites for their suggestion and urging to have my work published; and Sister Concetta, D.S.P., and the Daughters of St. Paul for their kind assistance in making this publication possible.

1. General Introduction

St. Teresa, the first woman to whom the title, Doctor of the Universal Church was given, is, according to *Butler's Lives of the Saints*, "one of the greatest, most attractive and widely appreciated women whom the world has ever known."[1] The personality of this remarkable woman retains a perennial charm. Her voice is not one of the remote past since she speaks from the pages of her books with the freshness of an author of the present time. The exalting favors which she received from God did not lift her from the mortal boundaries, instead they developed her natural qualities to their fullest maturity. Common sense, keen business ability, sparkling wit, warm-hearted sympathy, and understanding are some of the endearing traits which are manifested in St. Teresa. A genuine appeal to both the simple and the learned is harmoniously blended in her character of the natural and supernatural. As one who endured the conflicts of life and wrested from them the inner secrets of perfect peace, she will be ever venerated as an unsurpassable teacher of the art of prayer and a spiritual mother of souls.[2]

To this day whoever desires to know the spirit of Catholicism needs only to read her works. Written in obedience to her superiors, but with great personal reluctance, these books have piloted countless souls on the way to perfection. For some, St. Teresa's writings have even opened the door to conversion. The Protestant poet Crashaw, England's great baroque poet, embraced Catholicism and the priesthood after having read her works. Dr. Edith Stein, the renowned Jewish disciple of the philosopher Husserl, was so greatly influenced by the saint's writings that she became a nun in Teresa's own Order and died a martyr for her people in the gas chambers of Auschwitz. The historian Macaulay writes that St. Teresa by her life and writings "contributed more to stemming the tide of Protestantism than did Philip II and St. Ignatius Loyola." He also writes, "If Ignatius of Loyola is the brain of the Catholic reaction, Teresa of Jesus is its heart; if Ignatius is the head of a great band, Teresa of Jesus belongs completely to its humanity."[3]

The spiritual life of Europe was greatly influenced by Teresa's writings, especially French mysticism and the religious achievements of the seventeenth century. Saint Francis de Sales and St. Alphonsus Liguori, both Doctors of the Church, admired Teresa and turned to her works for guidance and inspiration. The non-Catholic world, as well, was influenced by her for centuries after her death:

> Johann Arndt, an important Protestant theologian and writer, was strongly influenced by her. Thomasius, one of the leaders of the German Enlightenment, made a profound study of her work. Gottfried Arnold, one of the leading Pietists, translated Teresa's writings. Tersteegen, the Protestant poet and mystic from the Lower Rhine, wrote an enthusiastic biography of her. The philosopher Leibniz looked up to her with respect, and admitted that she had stimulated his thinking.[4]

Realizing the desperate need of prayer in today's world, E. W. Trueman Dicken, an Anglican Priest, wrote an extensive study on the mysticism of St. Teresa and St. John of the Cross.[5] The Protestant theologian Walter Rigg calls

Teresa "one of the greatest women in history," and writes that "no words of praise can do her justice, for there is scarcely a comparison that she cannot support." He goes on to say that "we read Dostoevsky and Kafka, Pascal and Kierkegaard, and we are right to do so. But why do we not soak ourselves in the writings of Teresa? A really Christian outlook is hardly possible without them."[6]

Among the writings of St. Teresa, the following books can be indicated as the depositories of her spiritual teaching: her autobiography, the *Way of Perfection*, and the *Interior Castle*. Teresa wrote her autobiography primarily to manifest her spiritual state to her directors, but enlarged it by an addition devoted exclusively to the discussion of prayer. The *Way of Perfection* was written by Teresa for the purpose of teaching her nuns the major virtues that demand their concern, casting further light on the practice of prayer, and using the Our Father as a vehicle for teaching prayer at greater depth. This book is sometimes referred to as the "apex of Teresa's ascetical doctrine."[7] The *Interior Castle* is a purely mystical work in which she describes the seven stages through which the soul passes in order to attain mystical union with God. As Teresa's masterpiece, it is the principal source of mature Teresian thought on the spiritual life in its integrity.

A great amount of testimony in support of Teresa's authority can be produced from the Supreme Pontiffs. Teresa was beatified in 1614 by Paul V who inserted the phrase "let us be nourished by her celestial doctrine" into her liturgical prayer.[8] Eight years later at the celebrated canonization, March 12, 1622, Gregory XV inscribed Teresa in the list of saints, together with Ignatius Loyola, Francis Xavier, Isadore, the Farmer—all glories of Catholic Spain—and Philip Neri, a Florentine who lived in Rome.

Commemorating the Third Centenary of St. Teresa's Beatification, in a Letter of March 7, 1914, Pope St. Pius X did not hesitate to write:

> Whoever diligently reads her works will require no other treatises for living a truly holy life. For in these works this mistress of piety very clearly points out the safe way for advancing from the rudiments of the Christian life to the summit of holiness.... She teaches that true progress in prayer is above all else manifested by a more religious fulfillment of one's duties and a more earnest striving to act in a holy manner; and finally, that the more intimately one is mystically united with God, the more fervent becomes his exercise of charity toward others and the more solicitous he shows himself for the salvation of souls.[9]

On Sunday, September 27, 1970, Pope Paul VI conferred the title of Doctor of the Church on St. Teresa of Avila. In his homily on this occasion, the Pontiff described the "eminent doctrine" of the great 16th-century Spanish Carmelite as a doctrine which is summarized and exemplified in "her perennial, ever-present message—the message of prayer" which she bequested to the Church and the world. Her message, said the Pope, has great meaning for our own time since it is marked by a great effort at reform in the area of Christian prayer.[10]

This paper comes as the result of a life-long interest in the doctrine of St. Teresa. Over thirty years ago, as a young professed Sister, I came quite accidentally upon a copy of Walsh's biography of the saint. The charm and spiritual depth of Teresa had a pervading influence upon me, and her writings served as the basis for my religious life. With the passage of time I have found her to be even more appealing. In fact, one reason for pursuing theological studies was to become more familiar with her doctrine of prayer. Although a member of the Franciscan tradition, I have found the Carmelite Spirituality to be universal. Our Foundress, Mother Angela Truszkowska, urged us to take the Carmelite spirit of prayer as our own.

Pursuing the Carmelite spirit, I have had many experiences with the Carmelite way of life. Besides attending retreats and conferences conducted by Discalced Carmelites, I had the opportunity to spend thirty days at the Discalced Carmelite House of Prayer in Peterborough, New Hampshire, in June of 1974. Recalling the ancient Carmelite ideal of a remote, isolated community of members living as did the early hermits on Mount Carmel, the House of Prayer, up in the Monadnock Mountains, provided an atmosphere of silence, solitude, and contemplation punctuated by daily conferences in Scriptural and Carmelite Spirituality. I found the Peterborough experience to be invaluable because it not only gave me the opportunity to study the Carmelite tradition, but to live it as well.

Recently, I have maintained contact with the Carmelites by attending monthly conferences given for the members of the Third Order of Discalced Carmelites of Chicago. The tertiaries have inherited the full Carmelite tradition as is evidenced in the ideals of the Third Order:

> In the spirit of St. Teresa and St. John of the Cross, tertiaries are to be mindful of the presence of the Blessed Trinity in their persons. CARMEL means an enclosed or secret garden in which God Himself actually lives and dwells.
>
> The object of the Third Order is to make each tertiary conscious of the divine indwelling and to come as close as possible to Him, in this mortal life.
>
> Tertiaries, through Christian charity, are to bring the Guest into the lives of those with whom they live, work and socialize.[11]

Having been enriched by the above-mentioned Carmelite experiences in addition to my graduate theological studies, I gladly take this opportunity to analyze the Teresian Spirituality in depth and to present my findings in this study.

This thesis explores St. Teresa's doctrine of prayer and compares it with that of her contemporary, St. John of the Cross, and then attempts to show the relevance of Teresian Spirituality to man's current search for religious experience.[12]

Basically the divine indwelling in the soul is the foundation of Teresa's doctrine, which develops into a treatise on the growth and movement toward an end referred to as the transforming union with God. Outlined for clarity, not necessarily for chronological occurrence in the soul, the grades of Teresian prayer are explained in depth to familiarize the reader with the marks of progress by which St. Teresa identifies the steps through which she was led to the heights of mystical union. Paralleling the same doctrine is the Sanjuanist approach which supplements the other and occasionally presents alleged contradictions.

It is hoped that the perennial charm of Teresa and the clarity and depth of John of the Cross which constitute Teresian Spirituality[13] will penetrate the distance of four centuries and shed their light on contemporary man's search for the experience of God.

FOOTNOTES

1. *Butler's Lives of the Saints,* complete edition, edited, revised and supplemented by Herbert Thurston, S.J. and Donald Attwater, Vol. IV, (New York: P. J. Kennedy and Sons, 1956), 111. Reprinted with permission of Search Press, Ltd., for Burns and Oates, London.

2. Sister Mary Regina Lewis, O.C.D., *Saint Teresa of Jesus: Undaunted Daughter of Desires* (Long Beach, California: Carmel of St. Joseph, n.d.), 1.

3. Sebastian V. Ramge, O.C.D., *An Introduction to the Writings of St. Teresa* (Chicago: Henry Regnery Company, 1963), 16.

4. Gisbert Kranz, *Modern Christian Literature,* trans. from the French by J. R. Foster (New York: Hawthorn Books Publishers, 1961), 31. Reprinted with permission of E. P. Dutton, Inc.

5. E. W. Trueman Dicken, *The Crucible of Love: A Study of the Mysticism of St. Teresa of Jesus and St. John of the Cross* (New York: Sheed and Ward, 1963).

6. Kranz, *Modern Christian Literature,* 32.

7. S. V. Ramge, "St. Teresa of Avila," *New Catholic Encyclopedia,* (Washington: Catholic University of America, 1967) XIII, 1016.

8. Father Otilio Rodriguez, O.C.D., "Saint Teresa of Jesus: First Woman Doctor of the Church," xvi (Winter, 1970), 217.

9. John J. Sullivan, S.J., *God and the Interior Life* (Boston: St. Paul Editions, 1962), 108-109.

10. Pope Paul VI, "Teresa of Avila: The Message of Prayer," *The Pope Speaks,* XV (Autumn, 1970), 218-221. Reprinted with permission of *Our Sunday Visitor.*

11. "A Marian Way of Life," brochure describing the way of life of the Third Order of Discalced Carmelites, disseminated by the Discalced Carmelites of Milwaukee, 2.

12. Unless indicated otherwise, in citing the classics of the two Spanish Saints the following editions are used: *The Collected Works of St. Teresa of Avila,* Volume I copyright © 1976, Volume II copyright © 1980, translated by Kieran Kavanaugh and Otilio Rodriguez. ICS Publications, 2131 Lincoln Road, N.E. Washington, D.C. 20002. *The Collected Works of St. John of the Cross* translated by Kieran Kavanaugh and Otilio Rodriguez copyright © 1973 by Washington Province of Discalced Carmelites, Inc., ICS Publications, 2131 Lincoln Road, N.E., Washington D.C. 20002.

13. Father Gabriel of St. Mary Magdalen, O.C.D., "Characteristics of Teresian Spirituality," *Spiritual Life,* i (March, 1955), 37-38.

2. *The Teresian Doctrine of Prayer*

> There is no "need for wings to go to find Him. All one need do is go into solitude and look at Him within oneself."[1]

St. Teresa sought to find God in the depths of her own soul. Her whole doctrine of prayer consists in the movement towards God present in the soul, seeking thereby to be united perfectly with Him. According to the Carmelite authors, P. Marie-Eugene and Father Sebastian Ramge, the essential elements of her doctrine are:

1. the divine presence in the soul which is its fundamental truth;
2. growth in interior living which is its movement;
3. transforming union which is its end.[2]

The Divine Presence in the Soul

In her autobiography, we find St. Teresa saying: "It used to happen, when I represented Christ within me in order to place myself in His presence, or even while reading, that a feeling of the presence of God would come upon me unexpectedly so that I could in no way doubt He was within me or I totally immersed in Him."[3] Yet this interior certitude in regard to her own mystical experiences did not suffice for her. She questioned the truth of God's indwelling in the soul, "a truth," writes P. Marie-Eugene, "which was to be the basis of her whole spiritual teaching. She needs assurance of the teachings of faith and the conclusions of theology."[4]

St. Teresa looked for this assurance most diligently because she says: "I didn't know that God was in all things, and though He seemed so present to me, I thought this omnipresence was impossible. I couldn't stop believing that He was there since it seemed to me that I understood almost clearly that He was there by His very presence." She was greatly distressed because those who had no learning told her that "He was present only by grace."[5]

Fortunately, she met a Dominican Friar who assured her that He was indeed present and explained that besides being present supernaturally by grace, God is in all creatures in a threefold manner: first, by His power, inasmuch as all creatures are subject to Him; secondly, by His presence, because He sees all, even the most secret thoughts of the soul; thirdly, by His essence, since He acts everywhere and is the cause of the existence of all things, giving not only continual life and movement to His creatures, but their very being; and should God ever withdraw His presence, they would instantly cease to exist.[6] Having overcome this doubt, she was then able to state in the second chapter of the First Dwelling Places, that God is present in the soul, regardless of its moral condition through His divine immensity.[7]

It is interesting to note, that in some favored souls this divine experience is so clear, that through it they have come to sense the mystery of the divine presence even before they have learned anything about it.[8] Actually, St. Teresa's experience is a verification of the teaching of St. Thomas Aquinas, who writes: "By the gift of sanctifying grace, the rational creature is perfected so that it can freely use not only that created gift but even enjoy the divine Person Himself."[9]

It is at Baptism that this supernatural life of grace begins through the infusion of sanctifying grace. Moreover, this grace and its ancillary virtues endow the soul, supernaturally enabling it to live the divine life; it is through Baptism that the Blessed Trinity comes to dwell within the soul.

Furthermore, this doctrine of the indwelling is solidly witnessed in Sacred Scripture. To quote a few instances, St. John tells us, "Anyone who loves me will be true to my word, and my Father will love him; we will come to him and make our dwelling place with him."[10] In an exhortation to the Corinthians, St. Paul says: "You must know that your body is a temple of the Holy Spirit, who is within—the Spirit you have received from God. You are not your own. You have been purchased, and at a price. So glorify God in your body."[11] The apostle reminds the Galatians saying, "The proof that you are sons is the fact that God has sent forth into our hearts the spirit of his Son which cries out 'Abba!' ('Father!')."[12]

The entire New Testament, in fact, assumes the truth that the three Persons of the Blessed Trinity are substantially present in the soul of the just. God is now present in a new way, distinct from His presence by immensity; namely, He is present through bonds of friendship forged by the virtues of divine love and the object of faith and charity; with the growth of this divine intimacy, faith becomes more illumined and charity more vibrant.

As the Blessed Trinity lives its own intimate life within the soul endowed with sanctifying grace, the sanctified soul becomes in turn involved in some mysterious way within the very life that goes on within the Trinity itself. Thus the soul is enabled to live in the intimacy of the three Persons and to participate, although in a very limited manner, in the light and love of the Godhead itself.[13]

The meeting place of the soul with God is the very center of its own soul.[14] The more the soul corresponds and concentrates its powers and faculties on God within, the greater grows its divine life, even though the dynamism of this life may not be fully realized at first. However, every new grace brings with it a new presence of the Blessed Trinity, a new mission of the three Persons, by which the soul becomes more divinized, provided it continues to cooperate with this grace.[15] Thus the soul enters a more intimate relationship with the three Persons who, in turn, manifest Themselves ever more clearly to the faithful soul. St. Teresa explains from her own experience that her "soul was filled with the Godhead" like a sponge that is penetrated and saturated with water, "and in a certain sense it had within itself the fruition and the possession of the three Persons."[16]

When the soul experiences the divine indwelling in an ineffable manner, says St. Teresa, then, all that the soul knew and believed through faith, it now experiences as if by sight and touch. In the first chapter of the Seventh Dwelling Places she explains that the soul may be said here to grasp by sight—"although the sight is not with the bodily eyes nor with the eyes of the soul," because it is not an imaginative vision. By way of clarification she states that "here all three Persons communicate Themselves to it, speak to it, and explain those words of the Lord in the Gospel: that He and the Father and the Holy Spirit will come to dwell with the soul that loves Him and keeps His commandments."[17]

This testimony of St. Teresa corroborates from the field of experience the teaching of scholarly theologians, and is in full harmony with the Sacred Scripture on the divine indwelling.

Growth in Interior Living

In her *Interior Castle,* which the eminent scholar E. Allison Peers proclaims as "one of the most celebrated books on mystical theology in existence,"[18] St. Teresa expounds the concept of growth whereby the soul is oriented and moves towards its own depths. Each stage of progressive growth in interior living tends toward a progress in union with God.

St. Teresa begins this work by thinking of the soul "to be like a castle made entirely out of a diamond or of very clear crystal, in which there are many rooms, just as in heaven there are many dwelling places." These dwelling places are variously arranged—some are located above, others below, or on the sides of one another, but in the center and midst of them all is the most important dwelling place, where the most secret things transpire between God and the soul.[19]

Here the mystical figure of the dwelling places is used to trace the soul's progress from the First Dwelling Places to the Seventh, and its transformation from a sinful creature into the Bride of the Spiritual Marriage. The soul first enters the castle by means of prayer and meditation. And once inside, it is free to move about and is not constrained to stay for any length of time in any single room. However, because the soul must cultivate self-knowledge, it must "try to enter first into the room where self-knowledge is dealt with rather than fly off to other rooms. This is the right road."[20]

Moreover, for St. Teresa, the life of prayer is consistent with the life of virtue because, life of prayer, interior recollection, and intimacy with God progress simultaneously with growth in grace and moral virtue. The development of the interior life may best be portrayed by briefly describing each of the Seven Mansions.

In the First Mansions, St. Teresa considers the dignity and beauty of the human soul, made in the image and likeness of God and laments that we trouble so little about carefully preserving the soul's beauty. Even though in these mansions the soul is in a state of grace, it is still enmeshed in worldly pleasures, honors, and ambitions; therefore, it stays for a long time in the mansions of self-knowledge and humility, the very foundation for the spiritual life. However, it will never succeed in knowing itself unless it seeks to know God. It must set its eyes upon Christ from whom it shall learn true humility. St. Teresa explains that "the intellect will be enhanced...and self-knowledge will not make one" timorous and fearful. "Even though this is the first dwelling place it is very rich and...precious."[21]

Having finished its stay in the First Dwelling Places, the soul is now led on to the Second Dwelling Places in which it begins to practice prayer. Here, it becomes anxious to penetrate farther into the castle. It begins to understand the Lord's appeals which reach it in various ways, such as edifying conversations, sermons, the reading of good books; or through sicknesses and trials; or by means of truths which God directly teaches the soul while it is engaged in prayer. Although the soul is not yet completely free from the assaults of the evil one, nevertheless, its powers of resistance keep increasing. St. Teresa says: "The whole aim of any person who is beginning prayer...should be that he work and prepare himself with determination and every possible effort to bring his will into conformity with God's will." If he fails from time to time, let him not "become discouraged and stop striving to advance," for even out of his failures God will bring good. As for these beginners, St. Teresa advises that they place their trust, not in themselves, but in the mercy of God, and then "they will see how His Majesty brings them from the dwelling places of one stage to those of another" and sets them on safe ground so that even in this life "they shall enjoy many more blessings than one can desire."[22]

Referring to the souls in the Third Dwelling Places, St. Teresa notes that they are most desirous not to offend God; they spend much time in recollection; they practice works of charity towards others and lead a disciplined and well-ordered life.[23] However, they have not as yet made a total self-surrender to God because their love is still governed by reason and in consequence their spiritual progress is slow. Although they suffer from aridity, they are granted occasional glimpses into the remaining dwelling places by way of encouragement, in order that they may prepare to enter them.[24]

The Fourth Dwelling Places introduce the soul to the first stages of mystical prayer; that is, prayer of recollection and prayer of quiet. Here the active ascetic efforts of the soul give way before a more pronounced influence of God in passive contemplation. Having now tasted God's consolations, it gradually withdraws from earthly pleasures and finds itself improved in all the virtues and "will continue to grow if it doesn't turn back now to offending God."[25]

If the soul is generous enough to give itself completely to God, it will be led to the Fifth Dwelling Places—the prayer of union and the state of spiritual betrothal in which God betrothes Himself to the soul.[26] The author describes this state in the following manner: "God so places Himself in the interior of that soul that when it returns to itself it can in no way doubt that it was in God and God was in it...even though years go by without God's granting that favor again," it cannot forget it.[27] By using the famous simile of the silk-worm, St. Teresa elucidates how the soul to which God grants these favors can prepare itself to receive them.[28] However she states that God can enrich souls in many ways and bring them to these Mansions by various other paths.[29]

In the Sixth Dwelling Places, the soul becomes vividly aware of the presence of God within it and desires to be alone with Him. "That meeting left such an impression that the soul's whole desire is to enjoy it again." As the Lover and beloved grow in intimacy, the soul receives increasing favors, together with increasing trials. These trials may be purely exterior, such as bodily illness, abandonment by friends, misunderstanding, persecution, difficulties with confessors; or they may be interior trials which despite all the soul's efforts to conceal them, it is unable to do so. The interior sufferings are so great that "these others would seem small if the interior ones could be clearly explained." These afflictions are necessary in order to purify the soul and to prepare it for union with its Spouse in the Seventh Dwelling Places.[30]

Finally the soul reaches the spiritual marriage in the Seventh Dwelling Places. "This secret union takes place in the very interior center of the soul, which must be where God Himself is."[31] Here it has reached the culminating point of its interior growth—complete transformation characterized by ineffable and perfect peace. Beyond this there is no higher state, except that of the Beatific Vision in eternity.

Transforming Union

Just as there are many dwellings, so too, there are many degrees of divine union. St. Teresa aspires to a union in the very highest degree which "consists essentially in a complete union of the soul with God through a transformation that makes it like to Him; hence, the name of 'transforming union' or union by the likeness of love."[32] She compares this union with rain falling "from the sky into a river" whereby the rain and the river become one water; "a little stream" entering the sea from which it cannot be separated; or like a ray of "light" which passes through two different windows of a room and becomes one on entering.[33]

St. Teresa's great collaborator, St. John of the Cross, steeped as he was in the disciplines of Scholastic philosophy and theology, is very clear in his exposition of the nature of the union of the soul with God. In *The Ascent of Mount Carmel* he writes, that in contrast to God's substantial union which is in the purely natural order existing in every soul, there can also exist a transforming union which is supernatural in nature and can be produced only in souls that are in the state of grace. It is a participation in the divine life consisting of a perfect union of wills, resulting from the perfect conformity of the soul's will with the will of God. As soon as the soul completely rids itself of what is repugnant to the divine will, it becomes transformed in God through love.[34]

God communicates Himself most completely to the soul that has advanced farthest in love, that is, to the one most conformed to His will. The soul that has attained complete conformity and likeness of will has reached total supernatural union and transformation in God. However, perfect union cannot be attained without perfect purity. St. John illustrates this by saying that a ray of sunlight shining upon a clear and polished windowpane is able to illumine and transform it by its own light, but if the glass window is hazed or stained in any way, the sun's ray is unable to do so completely. The extent of illumination depends upon the condition of the windowpane, and not upon the ray of sunlight. If the window is entirely clean, the ray of the sun will illumine and transform it in such a way that the window will appear identical with the ray. Although the nature of the window is distinct from that of the ray of the sun, it can be said in a certain way, that the window and the sun's ray become one "by participation." Thus, the soul is like this window "upon which the divine light of God's being is ever shining, or better, in which it is always dwelling by nature."[35]

Purity in the soul renders it capable to receive God and become united with Him. As soon as a man wipes "away all the smudges and smears of creatures, by uniting his will perfectly to God's," the soul becomes at once illumined by and transformed in God. Then God communicates to the soul His supernatural being in a way that it appears "to be God Himself" and possesses "all that God Himself has."

Moreover, when God bestows this supernatural favor upon the soul, the union becomes so complete that "all the things of both God and the soul become one in participant transformation," and the soul seems to lose its identity, becoming divine indeed, by participation. Although its natural being is transformed, nevertheless, it is as distinct from God's being as it was before the union, just as the window that is illumined by the ray of sunlight "has an existence distinct from the ray."[36]

St. Teresa writes that this soul now longs for the will of God to the extent that "whatever His Majesty does" the soul "considers it to be for the best"; if He wills that it "should suffer, well and good"; if not, it "does not worry" itself "to death" as it did before. It very strongly desires to serve Him, to sing His praises, and to help every soul it can. For not only does the soul "not desire to die but" it desires "to live very many years suffering the greatest trials if through these" it can "help that the Lord be praised, even though in something very small."[37]

With all the power of her being St. Teresa aspired toward this supernatural union and transformation in God. Desiring to draw from the "living water" as directly as possible, she gave to her doctrine its force and its dynamism, its direction and its end. Thus St. Teresa of Avila becomes a beacon of light to those souls who thirst for God, and who are willing to give themselves entirely to Him, in order that they may be transformed by His love and do His will.

FOOTNOTES

1. *Way of Perfection*, 28; Kavanaugh-Rodriguez, II, 140-141.
2. P. Marie-Eugene, O.C.D., *I Want to See God: A Practical Synthesis of Carmelite Spirituality*, Vol. I, trans. by Sister M. Verda Clare, C.S.C. (Chicago: Fides Publishers Association, 1953), 17; Reprinted with permission of *U.S. Catholic*. Ramge, *An Introduction to the Writings of Saint Teresa*, 99.

3. *Life*, 10; Kavanaugh-Rodriguez, I, 74.

4. P. Marie-Eugene, *I Want to See God*, 18.

5. *Life*, 18; Kavanaugh-Rodriguez, I, 121.

6. *Summa* I, q. 8, a. 3.

7. *Interior Castle*, I, 2; Kavanaugh-Rodriguez, II, 289.

8. M. M. Philipon, O.P., *The Spiritual Doctrine of Sister Elizabeth of the Trinity*, trans. by a Benedictine of Stanbrook Abbey (Westminster, Maryland: The Newman Bookshop, 1947), 9-12; 47.

9. *Summa* I, q. 43, a. 3, and 1.

10. John 14:23. (NAB)

11. 1 Cor. 6:19-20.

12. Gal. 4:6.

13. Fr. Marcellus, O.D.C., "Friendship with the Blessed Trinity," *St. Teresa of Avila: Studies in Her Life, Doctrine and Times*, ed. by Father Thomas, O.D.C. and Father Gabriel, O.D.C. (Dublin: Clonmore and Reynolds, Ltd., 1963), 113-114. Reprinted with permission of Search Press, Ltd., London.

14. *Interior Castle*, VII, 1; Kavanaugh-Rodriguez, II, 430.

15. *Summa* I, q. 43, a. 6, ad 2.

16. *Spiritual Relations*, xviii, *The Complete Works of Saint Teresa of Jesus*, 3 vols. translated and edited by E. Allison Peers from the critical edition of P. Silverio de Santa Teresa, C.D. (New York: Sheed and Ward, Inc., 1946), I, 343. Reprinted with permission of Andrews ar.d McMeel, Inc.

17. *Interior Castle*, VII, 1; Kavanaugh-Rodriguez, II, 430.

18. Introduction to the *Interior Castle;* Peers, II, 189.

19. *Interior Castle*, I, 1; Kavanaugh-Rodriguez, II, 283.

20. *Interior Castle*, I, 2; Kavanaugh-Rodriguez, II, 292.

21. *Interior Castle*, I, 2; Kavanaugh-Rodriguez, II, 293.

22. *Interior Castle*, II, 1; Kavanaugh-Rodriguez, II, 301-302.

23. *Interior Castle*, III, 1; Kavanaugh-Rodriguez, II, 306.

24. *Interior Castle*, III, 2; Kavanaugh-Rodriguez, II, 312.

25. *Interior Castle*, IV, 3; Kavanaugh-Rodriguez, II, 332.

26. *Interior Castle*, V, 4; Kavanaugh-Rodriguez, II, 354.

27. *Interior Castle*, V, 1; Kavanaugh-Rodriguez, II, 339.

28. *Interior Castle*, V, 2; Kavanaugh-Rodriguez, II, 341-344.

29. *Interior Castle*, V, 3; Kavanaugh-Rodriguez, II, 350.

30. *Interior Castle*, VI, 1; Kavanaugh-Rodriguez, II, 359-364.

31. *Interior Castle*, VII, 2; Kavanaugh-Rodriguez, II, 433.

32. P. Marie-Eugene, *I Want to See God*, 28.

33. *Interior Castle*, VII, 2; Kavanaugh-Rodriguez, II, 434.

34. *Ascent*, II, v. 3: Kavanaugh-Rodriguez, 115-116.

35. *Ibid.;* 116-117.

36. *Ibid.;* 117-118.

37. *Interior Castle*, V, 3; Kavanaugh-Rodriguez, II, 439.

3. *The Grades of Teresian Prayer*

In defining prayer St. Teresa writes that, in her view, it "is nothing else than an intimate sharing between friends; it means taking time frequently to be alone with Him who we know loves us."[1] In prayer she says, "the important thing is not to think much but to love much."[2] She clearly emphasizes the affective element of prayer, firmly insisting on the notion of love. In order to clarify emphatically the dynamic character of love she writes: "Love of God does not consist in tears or in...delight and tenderness, which for the greater part we desire and find consolation in; but it consists in serving with justice and fortitude of soul and in humility."[3]

Teresian prayer is a dialogue, a loving conversation with God. Although it is principally affective, reflection cannot be excluded, since knowledge is the guide, leading love onwards insofar as it generates in man the conviction that God loves him. Since to pray is to love, the development of prayer occurs simultaneously with the growth of love, which in turn marks the progress in the spiritual life. Hence, the degrees of prayer described by St. Teresa in her writings correspond directly with the development of the spiritual life.[4]

It must be noted, however, that the divisions of prayer given by the saint in her various writings do not correspond exactly. In her *Life* she enumerates four degrees of prayer:

meditation, prayer of quiet, prayer of the sleep of the faculties, and prayer of union. In the *Way of Perfection* she devotes two chapters to the prayer of recollection. In her most mature work, the *Interior Castle,* St. Teresa says nothing of the prayer of the sleep of the faculties, but she adds to the grades of prayer the mystical marriage, the highest degree of the prayer of union, which she did not previously experience. Ultimately, her teaching on the degrees of prayer may be divided into the following general categories: discursive prayer, prayer of active recollection, prayer of quiet, and the prayers of union.

Discursive Prayer

The first degree of prayer by which the soul starts its way towards the divine intimacy is meditation. According to St. Teresa, mental prayer consists in "being aware and knowing that we are speaking, with whom we are speaking, and who we ourselves are who dare to speak so much with so great a Lord."[5]

According to St. Teresa, the most fruitful subject of meditation for beginners in prayer is the "life of Christ" in His mysteries and especially in the mystery of His Sacred Passion. However, she writes that "there are many souls that benefit more by other meditations.... For just as there are many mansions in heaven, there are many paths." Nevertheless they must not fail to reflect often "on the Passion and life of Christ from which has come and continues to come every good."[6]

It is of utmost importance that the soul places "itself in the presence of Christ" and grows "accustomed to being inflamed with love for His sacred Humanity. It can keep Him ever present and speak with Him, asking for its needs and complaining of its labors, being glad with Him in its enjoyments and not forgetting Him because of them, trying to speak to Him, not through written prayers but with words that conform to its desires and needs. This is an excellent way of making progress, and in a very short time."[7]

St. Teresa advises those who use their intellects a great deal and can extract many ideas and conceptions from one subject not "to pass the whole time thinking." It is better for them to place "themselves in the presence of Christ and, without tiring the intellect, speak with and delight in Him and not wear themselves out in composing syllogisms; rather, they should show Him their needs and the reason why He doesn't have to allow us to be in His presence."[8]

For those "who cannot engage in much discursive reflection with the intellect" or cannot keep their thoughts from wandering she suggests the rather slow recitation of some vocal prayer, for example the Our Father. "Represent the Lord Himself as close to you...teaching you" and then just "look at Him." Speaking from her own experience St. Teresa continues: "If you grow accustomed to having Him present at your side, and He sees that you do so with love and that you go about striving to please Him, you will not be able...to get away from Him; He will never fail you. He will help you in all your trials; you will find Him everywhere."[9]

St. Teresa's prudence led her to foresee days of ill health, fatigue, or some indisposition when one cannot concentrate. Counseling her nuns she says that the very suffering of anyone in this state will show her that she is not at fault and God will see the good will. She "should not grow anxious, which makes things worse or tire" herself "trying to put order into something that at the time doesn't have any." She should "just pray as best" she can.[10]

Another means suggested by St. Teresa is meditated reading. In her *Life* she tells us that during her eighteen years of aridities, she "never dared to begin prayer without a book." Often the mere fact that she had it herself was sufficient.[11] "I...assure you that if with care you grow accustomed to what I have said your gain will be so great that even if I wanted to explain this to you I wouldn't know how."[12]

In any case, St. Teresa's teaching is a reminder of what is truly essential in prayer, especially that it is a person-to-person contact between intimate, loving friends. "I consider that soul advanced who strives to remain in this precious company and to profit very much by it, and who truly comes to love this Lord to Whom we owe so much. This is an excellent way of making progress, and in a very short time." St. Teresa assures us that "this method of keeping Christ present with us is beneficial in all stages and is a very safe means of advancing in the first degree of prayer, of reaching in a short time the second degree, and of walking secure against the dangers the devil can set up in the last degrees."[13]

Prayer of Active Recollection

After writing about meditation in the *Way of Perfection,* St. Teresa warmly recommends another kind of prayer, much simpler and more profitable—the prayer of recollection. In a wide sense it can be called a second degree because in it recollection is more intense than in ordinary prayer and it begins a new phase in the growth of prayer.[14]

The essence of prayer of recollection consists in a conscious realization of the presence of God within us which results from our own efforts. St. Teresa notes that we can obtain it for ourselves, for it is "not something supernatural, but that it is something we can desire and achieve ourselves with the help of God." Further she states: "I know, if you try, that within a year, or perhaps half a year, you will acquire it, by the favor of God."[15]

Consequently, it is important to know what to do in order to practice this prayer. "The soul collects its faculties together and enters within itself to be with its God," writes

St. Teresa. Although in the beginning it may be trouble-some since the senses, imagination and intellect tend spontaneously toward exterior things, however, "the gain will be clearly seen; we will understand, when beginning to pray, that the bees are approaching and entering the beehive to make honey" without any effort on our part. The withdrawal of the powers has no other purpose than to favor a living intimacy with the Divine Master.[16]

In order to facilitate the prayer of recollection, Saint Teresa highly recommends cultivating the habit of the awareness of the presence of God within the soul. "Imag-ine...that in this palace dwells this mighty King Who has been gracious enough to become your Father; and that He is seated upon an extremely valuable throne, which is your heart.... What a marvelous thing, that He who would fill a thousand worlds...would enclose Himself in something so small." But being Lord "He is free to do what He wants, and since He loves us He adapts Himself to our size." However "it is very important not only to believe these truths but to strive to understand them by experience" for it is one of the best ways of "greatly slowing down the mind and recollecting the soul."[17]

Realizing the doubts of the beginner who feels dis-mayed at having to entertain such greatness, Teresa teaches that God can gradually enlarge the soul "to receive what He will place within it" and that "He has the power to make this palace a large one." However, the soul must be absolutely resolved to give it to Him for His own and empty it in "such a way that He can store things there or take them away as though it were His own property." Since He refuses to force our will, "He takes what we give Him; but He doesn't give Himself completely until we give ourselves completely."[18]

With regard to the ascetical preparation of the soul, St. Teresa is just as rigorous as St. John of the Cross. God does not work within the soul as He does "when it is totally

His without any obstacle," she says. "If we fill the palace with lowly people and trifles, how will there be room for the Lord with His court?"[19] Although she uses imagery in abundance, she does so only to assist our faith-perception of God's interior presence, believing that the required ascetical effort will follow. Recollection is conditioned more by faith and asceticism than by any mere imagination of presence.[20] "I understood well that I had a soul," writes St. Teresa, "but what this soul deserved and Who dwelt within it I did not understand because I had covered my eyes with the vanities of the world."[21]

In order that the prayer of recollection might be fruitful, it is necessary that the living intimacy of love between the soul and the Divine Master be maintained during the day. In this manner it will gradually pervade one's whole life. If this companionship can be recalled by the soul "even in the midst of occupations...for only a moment...doing so is very beneficial." St. Teresa counsels her nuns to make use "of one's senses for the sake of the inner life. If you speak, strive to remember that the One with whom you are speaking is present within. If you listen, remember that you are going to hear One who is very close to you when He speaks," and need never to withdraw from His companionship.[22]

The prayer of recollection has its advantages. In return for the time spent and effort exerted, the soul gains a certain power over the senses; it becomes their master to a certain degree, by calming them and keeping them from following their own impressions. "These souls are safer from many occasions" of sin, and the "fire of divine love is more quickly enkindled" in them. "Since they are so close to the fire, a little spark will ignite and set everything ablaze. Because there is no impediment from outside, the soul is alone with its God; it is well prepared for this enkindling."[23]

"I never knew what it was to pray with satisfaction," confessed St. Teresa, "until the Lord taught me this method.... I have always found so many benefits from this habit of recollection."[24] Anxious that her Sisters strive to attain this prayer, she assures them that "with this kind of prayer even though it may be vocal, ...the intellect is recollected much more quickly," and its Divine Master will teach it and "give it the prayer of quiet" more speedily "than He would through any other method it might use."[25]

Prayer of Quiet

With the prayer of quiet St. Teresa introduces us to the first form of contemplative prayer. "This prayer is something supernatural, something we cannot procure through our own efforts."[26] The theological fact that lies behind it is that this prayer depends solely upon the action of the gifts of the Holy Spirit which do not function because of our efforts.[27] In the distribution of His gifts, "the Lord gives when He desires, as He desires, and to whom He desires. Since these blessings belong to Him, He does no injustice to anyone."[28] However, God cannot fail to give Himself to the soul who seeks Him perseveringly and with determination.

St. Teresa distinguishes three phases in the development of the prayer of quiet: passive recollection, quiet proper, and sleep of the faculties.

Passive Recollection

Although St. Teresa treated of passive recollection in her early writings, it is not until the *Interior Castle* that she distinguishes it clearly from the prayer of quiet. A year previously the saint had described it in the *Relation* to Father Alvarez, as "the first kind of prayer I experienced which seems to be supernatural...one which despite all our efforts, cannot be acquired by industry or diligence...an interior recollection felt in the soul." A person in this state does not want to "hear nor understand anything but what is then occupying it—namely, the possibility of converse with God alone." In passive recollection "there is no loss of any of the senses or faculties, ...their activity is concentrated upon God. This will be easily understood by anyone to whom Our Lord has granted" this prayer.[29]

In the *Interior Castle* she writes that it is this state that leads into the prayer of quiet and "almost always" precedes it. "Without...wanting to do so," a person closes his eyes and desires solitude. "It seems that without any contrivance the edifice is being built" in which he can pray. "The senses and exterior things seem to be losing their hold because the soul is recovering what it had lost.[30]

"Don't think this recollection is acquired by the intellect striving to think about God within itself, or by the imagination imagining Him within itself," explains Saint Teresa. "Such efforts are good and an excellent kind of meditation because they are founded on a truth, which is that God is within us," and with His help, "it is something each one can do" for himself. It is, however, an excellent means of preparation for passive recollection; according to St. Teresa, the passing from the active to the passive recollection is a normal transition.

In the state of infused recollection the soul experiences a very powerful inclination to recollection and finds itself "inside the castle" before it has begun "to think of God." The understanding is able to meditate but it feels the need of simplifying its manner of communicating with God. Instead of reasoning about Him, it now lovingly abides in His presence. Nevertheless, "it doesn't come when we want it but when God wants to grant us the favor."

St. Teresa believes "that when His Majesty grants" this prayer, "He does so to persons who are already beginning to despise the things of the world," if not actually, then at least in desire. "He calls such persons especially so that they might be attentive to interior matters." She concludes by saying that "if we desire to make room for His Majesty, He will give not only this but more, and give it to those whom He begins to call to advance further."[31]

Quiet Proper

Having announced Himself by the prayer of passive recollection, the Lord "begins now to give us His Kingdom" in the prayer of quiet, in which He bestows the soul with "peace by His presence."[32]

"All the faculties are calmed," writes St. Teresa, "and the soul understands in another way, very foreign to the way it understands through the exterior senses, that it is now close to its God and that not much more would be required for it to become one with Him in union." Besides experiencing a great satisfaction in one's soul, a person also "feels the greatest delight in his body.... He feels so happy merely with being close to the fount that he is satisfied even without drinking. It doesn't seem there is anything else for him to desire."[33] We recall the words of St. Augustine: "You have made us for Yourself, O God, and our heart is restless until it rests in You."[34]

Although "the faculties are stilled," Teresa continues, it is only "the will...that is captive here."[35] It feels itself drawn by divine love into a restful silence while the intelligence is clothed in a new light which causes it to know God in a new way. It is not knowledge consisting of concepts which renders the soul capable of putting its idea of God into words, but rather of a light of experience, produced in the soul as a vivid feeling of the presence of God which is inexpressible. The soul recognizes at once that this knowledge of God is better than that derived from the ordinary process of reasoning.[36] St. Teresa refers to it as "the beginning of pure contemplation," that is, the knowledge without concepts based on love and experienced by the will.[37]

While the will is bound to God in recollection and quiet the other two faculties are free. At times the will is helped by the understanding and memory enabling it to enjoy its great blessing more and more.[38] Sometimes the understanding goes about "in search of many words and reflections with which to give thanks for this benefit and piling up its sins and imperfections so as to make itself realize that it does not deserve it," in this manner annoying the soul and disturbing the delightful quiet of the will. At other times "even speaking," writes the saint, "by which I mean vocal prayer and meditation—wearies it: it would like to do nothing but love. This condition lasts for some time, and may even last for long periods."[39]

In the Fourth Dwelling Places St. Teresa notes from observation that due to a lack of knowledge many persons who practice prayer suffer "terrible trials" because they do not understand themselves; and worry over "that which isn't bad at all but good" and think it "a serious fault." Hence they become melancholy, and their health declines, and they even abandon prayer completely not realizing that "the soul is perhaps completely joined with Him in the dwelling places very close to the center while the mind is on the outskirts of the castle suffering from a thousand wild and poisonous beasts, and meriting by this suffering." The saint explains that "just as we cannot stop the movement of the heavens," because "they proceed in rapid motion, so neither can we stop our mind." Therefore, "we should not be disturbed; nor should we abandon prayer."[40]

It may happen that when the soul is "in this degree of prayer so sublime" its thoughts may wander off "to the more foolish things of the world." Then, the saint advises to laugh "at the intellect as at a fool" and remain in the state of quiet. For thoughts "will come and go," but the "will is the ruler and the powerful one" and will recall them "after itself without your being disturbed," writes St. Teresa. But if it tries "to draw the intellect back by force...the strength it has against the intellect will be lost.... As the saying goes, whoever tries to grasp too much loses everything."[41] Thus, the prayer of quiet is paradoxically also a prayer of much restlessness.

The soul must proceed "gently and noiselessly" and "pay no attention to the intellect, for it is a grinding mill," St. Teresa explains.[42] "The will rejoices in its enjoyment" and no effort should be made by the soul "to understand how it enjoys the favor or what it enjoys; but it forgets itself during that time, for the One who is near it will not forget to observe what is fitting for it."[43]

Planted within the soul by Him, this prayer "is a little spark of the Lord's true love...that begins to enkindle the large fire that...throws forth flames of the greatest love of God which His Majesty gives to perfect souls." St. Teresa continues, "I should very much like to advise these souls to be careful not to hide the talent since it seems God desires to choose them to bring profit to many others, especially in these times when staunch friends of God are necessary to sustain the weak."[44] However, she also advises "to find more solitude so as to make room for the Lord and allow His Majesty to work as though with something belonging to Him."[45]

Besides leading a very recollected life, it is imperative to develop greater generosity and detachment. If God gives a soul such pledges it is a "sign that He wants to give it a great deal.... But if the Lord sees that after He places the kingdom of heaven in the soul's house this soul turns to earthly things He will...seldom grant it this favor, and then for just a short space of time."[46]

The prayer of quiet may at times continue even in the midst of daily occupations. Then the soul feels that in its activities "the best part is lacking, that is, the will" which is "united with its God, and leaves the other faculties free to be occupied in what is for His service—and they then have much more ability for this. But in worldly matters, these faculties are dull and at times as though in a stupor."

"This is a great favor for those to whom the Lord grants it; the active and the contemplative lives are joined," says St. Teresa. "The faculties all serve the Lord together: the will is occupied in its work and contemplation without knowing how; the other two faculties serve in the work of Martha. Thus Martha and Mary walk together."[47] However, the harmony of the active and contemplative life will be deeper and more lasting in the more advanced forms of mystical prayer.

Sleep of the Faculties

In her autobiography St. Teresa lists the sleep of the faculties as a distinct grade of mystical prayer which is superior to the prayer of quiet, but in the *Spiritual Relations V* she regards it as a gradual development of the prayer of quiet. Some authorities on Teresian works identify this prayer with the prayer of union which is dealt with in the Fifth Mansions, however, others in agreement with Saint Teresa, among whom is St. Francis de Sales, regard it as a most perfect form of the prayer of quiet.[48]

In this kind of prayer, the soul, in its profound recollection in God, is quite absorbed with a kind of drowsiness, hence the name, "sleep of the faculties." The powers of the soul remain as it were asleep with regard to the things of the world while the soul remains profoundly united with God. "This kind of prayer is a very apparent union of the whole soul with God. But seemingly His Majesty desires to give leeway to the faculties so that they may understand and rejoice in the many things He is accomplishing here," writes the saint. The soul has no desire for the pleasures of the world for it has within it all that it desires.[49]

The faculties still have a certain freedom of movement, which, however, are always oriented towards God. "One utters many words here in praise of God without thinking them up, unless it is the Lord who thinks them up; at least the intellect is worth nothing here. The soul would desire to cry out praises, and it is beside itself—a delightful disquiet." While in this state St. Teresa, "who though not a poet suddenly composed some deeply-felt verses," in which she exhaled her love and "heavenly madness" for her Lord and King.[50]

St. Teresa describes "another kind of union, which, although...not a complete union, is greater than the union just mentioned," one which God granted to her very often. "God takes to Himself the will and even the intellect...so that it might not engage in discourse but be occupied with rejoicing in Him.... The memory and imagination remain free and when they find themselves alone "carry on such a war that the soul is left powerless." Since the understanding gives the soul no or little assistance in what it presents to the imagination, these faculties "don't rest in anything but flit from one thing to the other; they are like little moths at night, bothersome and annoying." The saint notes that here we have a picture of "both our great misery" and a very clear one of "the tremendous power of God.... For the faculties that run loose weary and harm us so much; and those that are with His Majesty give us repose."

The remedy which she finally discovered, after having caused herself much fatigue for many years, is the one she spoke of when describing the prayer of quiet: "to pay no more attention to the memory than one would to a madman—leave it go its way, for only God can stop it.... The memory is unable—no matter what it does...to gather to itself the other faculties; rather, without any labor, they often make the memory come to them."[51] St. Teresa advises the person "to abandon oneself completely into the hands of

God." Since "it is given over entirely to the Lord," it can overlook itself completely and "let His Majesty treat it as His own."[52]

In all these types of prayer that St. Teresa described "the glory and repose of the soul is so great that the body very perceivably shares in that joy and delight; it does so 'very perceivably,' and the virtues" are very highly developed in it.[53] The various states of the prayer of quiet are distinguished from the prayer of union principally in that "the divine action does not take hold of the powers radically—rather, it takes possession of them as they go into action, uniting with the personal action of the soul in its movement toward Him," explains Father Ermanno. For this reason in the prayer of quiet "the soul feels God is 'near it' rather than exactly 'within it.' It is in the prayer of union that the soul feels the divine action descending into the very depths of its being."[54]

Prayers of Union

St. Teresa distinguishes three forms of the prayer of union in which God invades the soul by progressive stages and places it in a state of complete passivity which excludes any possibility of personal cooperation. The forms of this prayer are: simple union, spiritual betrothal and spiritual marriage.

Simple Union

The prayer of simple union is presented by St. Teresa as a deepening of preceding favors. In comparing it to the prayer of quiet she writes: "Don't think this union is...like the one I mentioned before," in which the soul neither thinks it is asleep nor does it feel awake. In this state all the faculties are asleep "to the things of the world and to ourselves."[55] Now, not only the will, but all the interior faculties including the memory and imagination are captivated. The soul "rejoices without understanding what it is rejoicing in." In this state of prayer "all the senses are occupied in this joy in such a way that none is free to be taken up with any other exterior or interior thing. In the previous degrees, the senses are given freedom to show some signs of the great joy they feel," but because of the union of all the faculties, the soul cannot communicate this rejoicing "while being in the prayer. And if it were able," she says, "then this wouldn't be union."[56]

The duration of this prayer is always short, not more than a half an hour.[57] "God so places Himself in the interior of that soul that when it returns to itself it can in no way doubt that it was in God and God was in it." It is not by vision nor by reasoning that the soul acquires the knowledge of God's presence but by its abiding conviction "that only God can place there."[58]

It is evident that in this kind of prayer the soul is absorbed in the contemplation of God dwelling within. When commenting on the words of the *Song of Songs: He brought me into the wine cellar,* St. Teresa writes:

> I understand this union to be the wine cellar where the Lord wishes to place us when He desires and as He desires. But however great the effort we make to do so, we cannot enter. His Majesty must place us there and enter Himself into the center of our soul. And that He may show His marvels more clearly He doesn't want our will to have any part to play, for it has been entirely surrendered to Him. Neither does He want the door of the faculties and of the senses to be opened, for they are all asleep. But He wants to enter the center of the soul without going through any door, as He entered the place where His disciples were when He said, *pax vobis;* or as He left the tomb without lifting away the stone. Further on you will see in the last dwelling place how His Majesty desires that the soul enjoy Him in its own center even much more than here.[59]

In this passage St. Teresa helps us to understand how progress in prayer involves interiorization and passivity. God now acts within the soul. It is within itself that the soul has fruition of God.

However, the soul does not really understand what is taking place. It knows that it loves God more than ever, but it does not know how. It feels and experiences the love of God, yet words fail it. The soul begins to experience a transformation which St. Teresa aptly describes by means of the allegory of the silkworm that encloses itself in its cocoon only to emerge a butterfly. "It now has wings. How can it be happy walking step by step when it can fly?" It is the same with the soul in the prayer of union. It cannot recognize itself any longer. It finds itself burning with the desire to praise the Lord; it discerns plainly its unworthiness; it longs to suffer great trials; it yearns for solitude; it wants God to be known by all men, and, therefore, it is deeply grieved when it sees God being offended by them.[60] In fact, the grace of union is not given for the soul's own sake only. "It always brings profit to other souls during the time that it continues to live virtuously; and they catch fire from its fire." Furthermore, one of the fruits of such prayer is an advance in zeal for the salvation of mankind.[61]

For as long as the prayer of union lasts, it consists in the complete possession of the soul by God, in a "union with the will of God; such a union that there is no division between Him and the soul, but one same will."[62] St. Teresa defines the will of God as being two things which the Lord asks: "love of His Majesty and love of our neighbor. These are what we must work for," she says. "By observing them with perfection, we do His will and so will be united with Him.... The most certain sign, in my opinion, as to whether or not we are observing these two laws is whether we observe well the love of neighbor." However, showing a great understanding of the weakness of human nature she adds: "I believe that...we will not reach perfection in the love of neighbor if that love doesn't rise from love of God as its roots.... When you see yourself lacking in this love...you have not reached union." Again St. Teresa shows how inter-related are the operations of prayer and virtue. Ever encouraging onward she continues: So "beg our Lord to give you this perfect love of neighbor. Let His Majesty have a free hand, for He will give you more than you know how to desire because you are striving and making every effort to do what you can about this love."[63]

In order to explain the prayer of union still further, St. Teresa introduces the nuptial allegory: "You've already often heard that God espouses souls spiritually.... And even though the comparison may be a coarse one I cannot find another that would better explain what I mean than the sacrament of marriage." However, "this spiritual espousal is different in kind from marriage, for in these matters that we are dealing with there is never anything that is not spiritual. Corporal things are far distant from them, and the spiritual joys the Lord gives when compared to the delights married people must experience are a thousand leagues distant." St. Teresa maintains that this prayer is a "matter of love united with love, and the actions of love are most pure and so extremely delicate and gentle that there is no way of explaining them, but the Lord knows how to make them very clearly felt."[64]

This prayer of union is but a prelude to the spiritual betrothal. "Here below when two people are to be engaged, there is discussion about whether they might meet together so as to become more satisfied with each other," writes St. Teresa. Likewise, the soul sees in a mysterious way who He is whom she is about to take as her Spouse. "Through the work of the senses and the faculties she couldn't in any way or in a thousand years understand what she under-stands here in the shortest time." The soul becomes so fired with love that she does her utmost not to thwart this Divine betrothal.[65] Nevertheless, she must still weather long periods of trial and be finally purified under the refining hand of God before obtaining from Him the union which will transform her completely.

Spiritual Betrothal

In the state of spiritual betrothal, or ecstatic union, the soul undergoes various intense sufferings because it is being transformed, and such an operation demands a profound purification of its being and powers. There are the criticisms and calumnies of men, interior doubts, bodily infirmities, the distrust of confessors, attacks by the devil, the desertion of friends, and the terrible feeling that God is about to abandon it. All these leave the soul weary and humiliated.[66] However, only time, patience, and God's will can alleviate these trials.

Nevertheless, the scene is not completely dark; for the Beloved, far from deserting her, rests in the depths of the soul. Immersed in her trials she does not see Him. Therefore, the Beloved invites her to discover Him within her by means of extraordinary favors such as impulses, enkindlings of love, locutions, etc. Besides being a compensation for the many trials, these graces are also efficacious means to lead the soul to betrothal.

The Beloved desires to enter into betrothal with the soul, but before He does so, He wants the soul to desire Him ardently. He, therefore, increases these desires, rousing them by means of *impulses* "so delicate and refined, for they proceed from very deep within the interior part of the soul." Sometimes it is awakened by His Majesty as though by a "falling comet. And as clearly as it hears a thunderclap, even though no sound is heard, the soul understands that it was called by God." He makes it feel His presence, "but He doesn't want to reveal the manner in which He allows Himself to be enjoyed. And the pain is great, although delightful and sweet." St. Teresa tells us that "here all the senses and faculties remain free of any absorption, wondering what this could be, without hindering anything or being able...to increase or take away that delightful pain."[67]

The Spouse may also "awaken" the soul by an *enkindling of love* which is a feeling that rises in the depths of the soul, with a "fragrance" that delights its whole being and reveals the presence of the Beloved. Unlike that which happens in the case of impulses there is nothing here that causes pain. "The soul is moved with a delightful desire to enjoy Him, and thereby it is prepared to make intense acts of love and praise of our Lord."[68]

"God has another way of awakening the soul. Although it somehow seems to be a greater favor than those mentioned, it can be more dangerous," writes St. Teresa. This awakening is effected by means of spiritual words or *locutions* "given to the soul. Some seem to come from outside oneself; others from deep within the interior part of the soul; others, from the superior part; and some are so exterior that they come through the sense of hearing, for it seems there is a spoken word." For example, just as "don't be distressed," or "it is I, fear not," is sufficient to calm a soul experiencing great interior disturbance, if these words bring "power and authority," calm the soul, and make a lasting impression, St. Teresa assures us that these are the "surest signs" that they come from God.[69]

When the divine call has been heard, the soul is led to the spiritual marriage by means of rapture, "elevation or flight of spirit, or transport.... These latter terms, though different, refer to the same thing; it is also called *ecstasy*," writes St. Teresa. The grace of ecstasy opens up the state of betrothal which is the result of the soul's union with the Beloved. It differs from simple union in that it "produces much stronger effects and causes many other phenomena.... Since these other phenomena are of a higher degree, they produce their effect both interiorly and exteriorly," whereas simple union "seems the same at the beginning, in the middle, and at the end; and it takes place in the interior of the soul."[70]

The various forms of ecstasy are described by the saint with great precision. "One kind of rapture is that in which the soul even though not in prayer is touched by some word it remembers or hears about God." This causes a spark to increase, and burst into flame. "All burnt up, the soul is renewed like the phoenix, and one can devoutly believe that its faults are pardoned," writes the saint. Although "the faculties are so absorbed that we can say they are dead...the soul was never so awake to the things of God nor did it have such deep enlightenment and knowledge of His Majesty."[71]

"There is another kind of rapture...*flight of the spirit* which, though substantially the same as other raptures, is interiorly experienced very differently." Ecstasy, is, as a rule, sweet and peaceful and the powers are suspended gradually. On the contrary, the flight of the spirit is sudden, violent, and impetuous. The principal graces which the soul now receives are, according to St. Teresa, "knowledge of the grandeur of God,...self-knowledge and humility...and little esteem of earthly things save for those that can be used for the service of so great a God."[72] God gives these souls "the strongest desire not to displease Him" even by the least imperfection. "For this reason alone, if for no other, the soul wants to flee people, and it has great envy of those who have lived in deserts."[73]

St. Teresa describes another grace which the soul receives during the betrothal as that of jubilation: "It is, in my opinion, a deep union of the faculties; but our Lord nonetheless leaves them free that they might enjoy this joy—and the same goes for the senses—without under-standing what it is they are enjoying or how they are enjoying." The joy that wells up from the depths of the soul's being brings it such peace and happiness that the soul cannot contain itself in silence: so it calls upon all to praise

God. Sometimes when the soul experiences this grace it might be thought mad as was St. Francis when he was met by robbers on the countryside. "Oh what blessed madness, Sisters! If only God would give it to us all!"[74]

The *intellectual vision* is a further gift, a new kind of communication of love. By this grace the soul "will feel Jesus Christ, our Lord, beside it. Yet, it does not see Him, either with the eyes of the body or with those of the soul.... It isn't like the imaginative one that passes quickly, but lasts many days and sometimes even more than a year," writes St. Teresa. "This continual companionship...bears with it a particular knowledge of God...a most tender love for His Majesty," deeper yearnings "to surrender oneself totally to His service," and a "great purity of conscience." The soul would exchange this favor for no earthly treasure or joy. However, when the Lord is pleased to withdraw His presence, "the soul feels very much alone. But all the efforts it could possibly make are of little avail in bringing back that companionship. The Lord gives it when He desires, and it cannot be acquired."[75]

Although they are inferior to the ecstatic intellectual visions bestowed by the Lord in the final Mansions, the *imaginary visions* are in a certain sense "more beneficial because they are in greater conformity with our nature.... When our Lord is pleased to give more delight to this soul, He shows it clearly His most sacred Humanity in the way He desires; either as He was when He went about in the world or as He is after His resurrection." Although this happens as quickly as a flash of lightning, the image is so deeply engraven upon the imagination that it cannot possibly disappear "until it is seen by the soul in that place where it will be enjoyed without end." One does not look at the vision as at a "painting," explains St. Teresa, "but truly alive," the Lord speaks to the soul and even reveals "great secrets." The brilliance of the vision "is like that of the infused light coming from a sun covered by something as transparent as a properly cut diamond.... Almost every time God grants this favor the soul is in rapture." These visions bring the recipient "true Wisdom" without any effort on its own part, an increase in humility, and a strengthening in virtue.[76]

The rich mystical graces experienced during this stage of spiritual betrothal show the various forms under which the Spouse visits the soul. However, the perfection of mystical prayer does not depend on these graces, but rather in contemplation. "Contemplation of itself does not require any extraordinary manifestations of supernatural realities; rather it causes them to be tested through an experimental knowledge which gives an inexpressible sense of God."[77] St. Teresa warns: "Although this path may seem to you very good, one to be highly esteemed and reverenced," you must never ask or desire Him to lead you this way. She advises that we should rather "place ourselves in His hands so that His will may be done in us, and we cannot err if with a determined will we always maintain this attitude."[78]

Unlike the majority of the mystics and theologians of the time, St. Teresa taught that the path leading to the most exalted contemplation must be the Humanity of Christ. "God desires that if we are going to please Him and receive His great favors," she writes, "we must do so through the most sacred Humanity of Christ, in whom He takes His delight.... We must enter by this gate if we desire His sovereign Majesty to show us great secrets." Therefore, even if we reach the summit of contemplation we must seek no other way; "on this road you walk safely." The soul needs to have something to lean upon no matter how full it may think itself to be of God. Unless God, Himself, suspends all the faculties and takes this Presence away from us, we must always strive to keep this most sacred Humanity of Christ ever before us.[79] For the Lord Himself says, "I am the way, and the truth, and the life; no one comes to the Father but through me."[80]

Towards the end of the ecstatic union the soul undergoes still greater sufferings of a purifying and passive
nature; this is the final purification for the mystical
marriage. "When our Lord is pleased to have pity on this
soul that He has already taken spiritually as His spouse
because of what it suffers and has suffered through its
desires," He comes to visit her in that final rapture and
ecstasy of delight which introduces her into the state of
spiritual marriage.[81]

Spiritual Marriage

Before consummating the spiritual marriage, God
brings the soul into His own dwelling place by means of an
intellectual vision in which the soul sees the three Persons of
the Blessed Trinity communicating Themselves to it. "First
there comes an enkindling in the spirit in the manner of a
cloud of magnificent splendor." The soul sees these three
Persons to be distinct, yet by a wonderful kind of knowledge that is given to it, the soul knows with an absolute
certainty that all the three Persons are of one substance, one
Power, one Knowledge, and one God Alone: "that what
we hold by faith, it understands, we can say, through
sight—although the sight is not with the bodily eyes nor
with the eyes of the soul, because we are not dealing with an
imaginative vision. Here all three Persons communicate
Themselves to it, and explain those words of the Lord in the
Gospel: that He and the Father and the Holy Spirit will
come to dwell with the soul that loves Him and keeps His
commandments." Every day "this soul becomes more
amazed, for these Persons never seem to leave it any more,"
and now perceives quite clearly that They are within it—in
the extreme interior—in some place very deep within
itself.[82]

Although this Presence is not always realized clearly
and to the full, "the soul finds itself in this company every

time it takes notice." She is sure of Their Presence in the way one is sure of the presence of friends in a room although all of a sudden the shutters are closed. Then one feels the presence of the friends even though they cannot be seen. To see more clearly the soul has to wait until "our Lord desires that the window of the intellect be opened. Great is the mercy He shows in never departing from the soul," exclaims St. Teresa, "and in desiring that it perceive Him so manifestly."[83]

The experience of the indwelling Trinity and of the nearness and intimacy of God does not prevent her from action or distract her from external occupations. The soul is not completely absorbed, and in fact, "is much more occupied than before with everything pertaining to the service of God; and once its duties are over it remains with that enjoyable company. If the soul does not fail God, He will never fail...to make His presence clearly known to it" by means of which He desires to prepare her for greater favors.[84]

When granting the favor of the spiritual marriage, writes St. Teresa, "His Majesty desires to show Himself to the soul through an imaginative vision of His most sacred Humanity so that the soul will understand and not be ignorant of receiving this sovereign gift." However, she says: "With other persons the favor will be received in another form."[85]

Nevertheless, the spiritual marriage takes place in the innermost center of the soul, the dwelling place of God Himself, and into which He enters without the medium of the senses or faculties. In the graces previously described, the senses and the faculties are in some sense used as intermediaries, but what takes place in the union of the spiritual marriage is very different. The Lord appears in the deepest center of the soul without any imaginative vision but by means of an intellectual vision still more refined than those of which the saint has spoken thus far. This communication of God is so sublime and so delightful to the soul that it can only be compared to the "glory that is in Heaven" which surpasses all visions and all spiritual consolations.[86]

The experience of the union of the soul with God is permanent in the spiritual marriage. This is what differentiates this degree of prayer from all the rest in which the union is conscious only from time to time. The other graces of prayer are like "spiritual betrothals" in which the favor of union is intermittent. On the contrary in the spiritual marriage, St. Teresa says, "the soul always remains with its God in that center."[87]

Turning to the Scriptures the saint writes that probably when St. Paul says: "Whoever is joined to the Lord is one spirit with Him,"[88] he is referring to the union of the mystical marriage. Then commenting on the passage, "For, to me, 'life' means Christ; hence dying is so much gain,"[89] she applies these words to the soul that is now dead to its natural way of living, but lives a new life because within her lives Christ.[90]

With the passing of time the soul clearly understands, by certain secret aspirations, that it is endowed with the life of God. "These aspirations come very, very often in such a living way that they can in no way be doubted. The soul feels them very clearly even though they are indescribable." St. Teresa tries to explain these operations with a comparison to a great stream of water that could never fall on us without having an origin somewhere. In the same way "it is understood clearly that there is Someone in the interior depths who shoots these arrows and gives life to this life, and that there is a Sun in the interior of the soul from which a brilliant light proceeds and is sent to the faculties."[91]

Upon reaching this state the ecstasies usually cease. The great weakness which previously was the occasion for raptures is now replaced by a great strength which is granted by the Lord; nevertheless, the soul walks with great care and humility "so as not to abandon through their own fault any opportunity to please God more." Aridities and interior trials give way to a tender love for Him who is within. Action and contemplation are no longer in contrast, but are fully identified. The soul has a great desire to suffer, and if it is the victim of persecution it bears no enmity toward those who treat it badly. The soul is now totally forgetful of itself "because it employs all it has in procuring the honor of God." It is now completely transformed.[92]

"I tell you," writes St. Teresa, "that the cross is not wanting," but it never loses its peace. "For the storms like a wave, pass quickly. And the fair weather returns." The dove returns to the ark. All is stillness; all is peace. "Here one delights in God's tabernacle" awaiting the day when it will behold Him face to face for all eternity.[93]

This is the Teresian prayer: a journey from asceticism to mysticism, from meditation to contemplation—a prayer which has as its beginning and end our Lord in His sacred Humanity and the Blessed Trinity. This prayer, which is decidedly Christocentric and Trinitarian, is eminently Christian.

FOOTNOTES

1. *Life*, 8; Kavanaugh-Rodriguez, I, 67.
2. *Interior Castle*, IV, 1; Kavanaugh-Rodriguez, II, 319.
3. *Life*, 11; Kavanaugh-Rodriguez, I, 84.
4. Fr. Ermanno O.D.C., "The Degrees of Teresian Prayer," *St. Teresa of Avila: Studies in Her Life, Doctrine and Times*, ed. by Father Thomas, O.D.C. and Father Gabriel, O.D.C. (Dublin: Clonmore and Reynolds, Ltd., 1963), 78. Reprinted with permission of Search Press, Ltd., London.
5. *Way of Perfection*, 25; Kavanaugh-Rodriguez, II, 131.
6. *Life*, 13; Kavanaugh-Rodriguez, I, 93.
7. *Life*, 12; Kavanaugh-Rodriguez, I, 86.
8. *Life*, 13; Kavanaugh-Rodriguez, I, 92-93.
9. *Way of Perfection*, 26; Kavanaugh-Rodriguez, II, 133-134.
10. *Way of Perfection*, 24; Kavanaugh-Rodriguez, II, 130.
11. *Life*, 4; Kavanaugh-Rodriguez, I, 44.
12. *Way of Perfection*, 26; Kavanaugh-Rodriguez, II, 137.

13. *Life,* 12; Kavanaugh-Rodriguez, I, 86.

14. Father Gabriel of St. Mary Magdalen, O.C.D., *The Way of Prayer,* trans. by The Carmel of Baltimore (Milwaukee: Spiritual Life Press, 1965), 95; Ermanno, "The Degrees of Teresian Prayer," 82.

15. *Way of Perfection,* 29; Kavanaugh-Rodriguez, II, 147 and 149.

16. *Way of Perfection,* 28; Kavanaugh-Rodriguez, II, 141-143.

17. *Ibid.,* 143-144, 140.

18. *Ibid.,* 144-145.

19. *Ibid.*

20. Fr. Norbert O.D.C., "The Prayer of Active Recollection According to St. Teresa," *St. Teresa of Avila: Studies in Her Life, Doctrine and Times,* ed. by Father Thomas, O.D.C. and Father Gabriel, O.D.C. (Dublin: Clonmore and Reynolds, Ltd., 1963), 108. Reprinted with permission of Search Press, Ltd., London.

21. *Way of Perfection,* 28; Kavanaugh-Rodriguez, II, 144.

22. *Way of Perfection,* 29; Kavanaugh-Rodriguez, II, 147-148.

23. *Way of Perfection,* 28; Kavanaugh-Rodriguez, II, 142-143.

24. *Way of Perfection,* 29; Kavanaugh-Rodriguez, II, 148.

25. *Way of Perfection,* 28; Kavanaugh-Rodriguez, II, 141.

26. *Way of Perfection,* 21; Kavanaugh-Rodriguez, II, 153.

27. Gabriel of St. Mary Magdalen, *Way of Prayer,* 105.

28. *Interior Castle,* IV, 1; Kavanaugh-Rodriguez, II, 317.

29. *Spiritual Relations,* V; Peers, I, 327.

30. *Interior Castle,* IV, 3; Kavanaugh-Rodriguez, II, 327.

31. *Ibid.;* 328-329.

32. *Way of Perfection,* 31; Kavanaugh-Rodriguez, II, 153.

33. *Ibid.;* 153-154.

34. St. Augustine, *The Confessions of St. Augustine,* trans., with an Introduction and Notes, by John K. Ryan (Garden City, New York: Image Books of Doubleday & Company, Inc., 1960), 43.

35. *Way of Perfection,* 31; Kavanaugh-Rodriguez, II, 153.

36. Ermanno, "The Degrees of Teresian Prayer," 89.

37. *Way of Perfection,* 30; Kavanaugh-Rodriguez, II, 151-152.

38. *Way of Perfection,* 31; Kavanaugh-Rodriguez, II, 154.

39. *Spiritual Relations,* V; Peers, I, 328.

40. *Interior Castle,* IV, 1; Kavanaugh-Rodriguez, II, 320.

41. *Way of Perfection,* 31; Kavanaugh-Rodriguez, II, 158.

42. *Life,* 15; Kavanaugh-Rodriguez, II, 104.

43. *Way of Perfection,* 31; Kavanaugh-Rodriguez, II, 157.

44. *Life,* 15; Kavanaugh-Rodriguez, I, 103-104.

45. *Way of Perfection,* 31; Kavanaugh-Rodriguez, II, 156.

46. *Ibid.;* 158-159.

47. *Ibid.;* 155.

48. St. Francis de Sales, *The Love of God: A Treatise,* trans. and intro. by Vincent Kerns (Westminster, Maryland: The Newman Press, 1962), 24.

49. *Life,* 17; Kavanaugh-Rodriguez, I, 113.

50. *Life,* 16; Kavanaugh-Rodriguez, I, 109-110.

51. *Life,* 17; Kavanaugh-Rodriguez, I, 114-115.

52. *Ibid.;* 112.

53. *Ibid.;* 115.

54. Ermanno, "The Degrees of Teresian Prayer," 92.

55. *Interior Castle,* V, 1; Kavanaugh-Rodriguez, II, 336.

56. *Life,* 18; Kavanaugh-Rodriguez, I, 116-117.
57. *Ibid.;* 121.
58. *Interior Castle,* V, 1; Kavanaugh-Rodriguez, II, 339.
59. *Ibid.;* 340.
60. *Interior Castle,* V, 2; Kavanaugh-Rodriguez, 341-344.
61. *Interior Castle,* V, 3; Kavanaugh-Rodriguez, 348.
62. *Meditations on the Song of Songs,* 3; Kavanaugh-Rodriguez, II, 236.
63. *Interior Castle,* V, 3; Kavanaugh-Rodriguez, II, 351-353.
64. *Interior Castle,* V, 4; Kavanaugh-Rodriguez, II, 354.
65. *Ibid.;* 355.
66. *Interior Castle,* VI, 1; Kavanaugh-Rodriguez, II, 360-364.
67. *Interior Castle,* VI, 2; Kavanaugh-Rodriguez, II, 367-368.
68. *Ibid.;* 370.
69. *Interior Castle,* VI, 3; Kavanaugh-Rodriguez, II, 370-373.
70. *Life,* 20; Kavanaugh-Rodriguez, I, 129. (Italics mine.)
71. *Interior Castle,* VI, 4; Kavanaugh-Rodriguez, II, 379-380. (Italics mine.)
72. *Interior Castle,* VI, 5; Kavanaugh-Rodriguez, II, 386-390. (Italics mine.)
73. *Interior Castle,* VI, 6; Kavanaugh-Rodriguez, II, 392.
74. *Interior Castle,* VI, 6; Kavanaugh-Rodriguez, II, 395-396.
75. *Interior Castle,* VI, 8; Kavanaugh-Rodriguez, II, 405-408.
76. *Interior Castle,* VI, 9; Kavanaugh-Rodriguez, II, 410-414.
77. Ermanno, "The Degrees of Teresian Prayer," 92.
78. *Interior Castle,* VI, 9; Kavanaugh-Rodriguez, II, 416-417.
79. *Life,* 22; Kavanaugh-Rodriguez, I, 146-148.
80. John 14:6.
81. *Interior Castle,* VII, 1; Kavanaugh-Rodriguez, II, 428.
82. *Ibid.;* 430.
83. *Ibid.;* 431.
84. *Ibid.*
85. *Interior Castle,* VII, 2; Kavanaugh-Rodriguez, II, 432.
86. *Ibid.;* 433-434.
87. *Ibid.*
88. 1 Cor. 6:17.
89. Phil. 1:21.
90. *Interior Castle,* VII, 2; Kavanaugh-Rodriguez, II, 434-435.
91. *Ibid.*
92. Cf. *Interior Castle,* VII, 3; Kavanaugh-Rodriguez, II, 438-443.
93. *Ibid.;* 442-443.

4. A Comparison of St. Teresa of Avila and St. John of the Cross on Their Doctrine

Is it possible to think of St. Teresa of Avila without being reminded of her great collaborator, St. John of the Cross? Hardly. They were closely associated in their life's work and in their writings. Their books were written primarily for the practical purpose of guiding souls of good will to the heights of divine union. It was the genius of St. Teresa to formulate her doctrine from a psychological and motherly point of view. The scholastic training and the scientific mind of St. John of the Cross enabled him to systematize her teachings. Thus the two Mystical Doctors of the Church, by complementing each other, have reached the heights of Western Mystical Theology which to date have not been surpassed.

The Treatises of St. John of the Cross

St. John of the Cross wrote three major doctrinal treatises: *The Ascent of Mount Carmel—The Dark Night, The Spiritual Canticle,* and *The Living Flame of Love*. These writings have greatly influenced studies in spiritual theology. In proclaiming St. John of the Cross a Doctor of the Universal Church in 1926, Pius XI asserted that they may be rightly called a code and guide for all seeking to live a more perfect life.

Beginning as a commentary on the poem, "The Dark Night," *The Ascent of Mount Carmel—the Dark Night* is a treatise describing the journey of a soul on its way toward union with God. This journey is referred to as a dark night because the person on this path "must deprive himself of his appetite for worldly possessions"; travel the path of faith; and receive God's communications. These reasons involve privation just as night involves a privation of light.[1]

The *Ascent* is divided into three books and the *Dark Night,* into two.

In Book One of the *Ascent* St. John of the Cross discusses the mortification of all voluntary, inordinate appetites for creatures, since these appetites are contrary to the perfect love of God and consequently to union with the Divine. He also refers to the active night of the senses instructing that a man must acquire the habit of using his sense faculties only for the honor and glory of God, and "have a habitual desire to imitate Christ" in all his deeds by bringing his life "into conformity with His."[2]

Books Two and Three of the *Ascent* treat of the journey in faith, especially as it is in the active purification of the spirit. In order to reach union with God, the soul must walk in the darkness of faith. It must also deprive itself of everything which is not in perfect conformity with the full adherence to God and to the law of Christ and of His Church. In the active night of the spirit, a man must strive to purify his spiritual faculties by means of the theological virtues. St. John of the Cross explains how each of these virtues purifies its respective faculty of whatever is not for God's glory and unites it to God. In these two books he has in mind "those especially who have begun to enter the state of contemplation."[3] In endeavoring to purify their spiritual faculties they must also turn aside in prayer from particular knowledge in order to receive through a general loving attentiveness in faith, the general loving knowledge of God which is contemplation.

In the two books of the *Dark Night* the Mystical Doctor describes how God purifies the soul passively and brings its faith and love to the perfection portrayed in the *Ascent*. The discussion of God's communication is limited to the contemplation which purifies and perfects the soul in the passive nights of the senses and of the spirit. Because this contemplation is dark and painful to the soul it is called a night.

Book One of the *Night* deals with the imperfections which weigh upon beginners, the signs of initial contemplation, and the transition from the state of beginners to the state of proficients. It also treats of the benefits of the passive purifications of the senses.

Book Two describes the proficient's state of soul and explains the time in which God places one in the passive night of the spirit. It treats of the necessity of the passive purifications of the spirit and gives a vivid picture and analysis of the purgative contemplation that God infuses during this night.

By means of the active and passive purifications, the soul reaches union with God, divesting itself of everything that is not in conformity with His will. In this union, it habitually utilizes all its faculties, appetites, operations, and emotions in God, so that in its activity it resembles God; this union is called "the union of likeness."[4]

The Spiritual Canticle, comprised of a poem and a commentary, is a colloquy of love between the Mystical Doctor and Christ. The outpourings of this love are the result of the abundant mystical understanding which was communicated to his soul by his Beloved. Due to the high mystical experience of St. John of the Cross and the ineffableness of that experience, the lyric verses of the *Canticle* were the best means he could find to set in words that which in itself remained beyond words.

In recounting the history of his love of Christ, St. John marks the degrees and stages of his spiritual life. In its general plan the poem dwells on four main aspects of the life of divine love:

1) the anxious loving search for the Beloved;
2) the first encounter with Him, the spiritual espousal, and the life of union with Him which is not yet perfect;
3) perfect union with the Bridegroom, or, the spiritual marriage, and the life of love in this state of perfection;
4) the desire for the perfect union with and transformation in the Beloved in glory.[5]

The love that constitutes the core of the poem is essentially dynamic and is conceived as an uninterrupted progression in sanctity. The progression corresponds not only to the personal experience of St. John, but also in its general plan to the common path which leads to spiritual perfection.

The Living Flame of Love is also a poem with a commentary. This poem is the song of a soul that has reached a highly perfect love within the state of transformation. The state of transformation in God is the loftiest attainable on earth. It is equivalent to the state called "spiritual marriage" in the *Canticle:* "This spiritual marriage...is a total transformation in the Beloved.... It is accordingly the highest state attainable in this life."[6] It can also be equated with the divine union and "transformation of the soul in God" called "the union of likeness," the goal toward which the soul is directed in the *Ascent-Night.*[7] Thus, whether St. John refers to the highest degree of perfection as the divine union, the spiritual marriage or the state of transformation, the reality is the same: a union with

God through the likeness of love. It is by means of this union that man becomes consciously united to the divine Trinity in the very substance of his soul; his understanding is divinely enlightened by the wisdom of the Son, the will is gladdened by the Holy Spirit, and the Father with His power and strength absorbs the soul in the embrace of sweetness.[8]

In his major doctrinal works, therefore, St. John of the Cross treats mainly of how one reaches union of God, and of the life of divine union itself. Briefly, this union is reached through the practice of the theological virtues, which purify the soul and unite it with God. The life of union with God is a life of perfect faith, hope, and charity.

In comparing some of the similarities and diversities that are found in the doctrine of St. John and St. Teresa, the division employed by Father Gabriel in his study will be used, namely:

1. points of substantial agreement;
2. points in which St. John notably supplements St. Teresa;
3. points in which St. Teresa notably supplements St. John;
4. alleged contradictions between the two.[9]

Points of Substantial Agreement

The whole of the doctrine taught by St. Teresa and St. John of the Cross is founded on Sacred Scripture and the dogmatic teaching of the Church. The four doctrines that stand out in particular are: the revealed teaching about God's being and attributes; man's nature and supernatural destiny; the disruption caused in man's nature by sin, original and personal; man's redemption and sanctification in Christ and through the Church. However, they rarely refer to these doctrines explicitly. Instead, they take for granted that the dogmatic teaching is known, and draw certain conclusions as to the relations between the soul and God and the means that men must use to be united with God. "Their doctrine is the distilled essence of Christianity, a practical application of the Church's teaching on the theological virtues and grace."[10]

The goal of the spiritual life, too, is the same for them both; namely, the summit of divine union in which the human will is totally united with the divine, and the understanding and memory transformed in faith and hope. All else concerns the means that lead up to this, or the accidents that accompany it, or the effects that follow from it.[11] It is interesting to note that just as St. Teresa uses the symbols of a castle and its mansions as a vehicle to describe the path which leads to spiritual fulfillment in God, in like manner, St. John of the Cross uses the symbolism of Solomon's *Canticle* to point out the way to the heights of mystical union with his Beloved.

Although the Carmelite Doctors speak from the abundance of their own experience in mapping out a direct and safe way to the goal of divine union, they are careful, nonetheless, not to limit the possible work of God to that which they describe. This is particularly true of St. Teresa who writes: "It is important to understand that God doesn't lead all by one path."[12] Likewise, both of them stress the fact that human reason must be used in its own sphere, in the soul's ascent to God. "One thought alone of man is worth more than the entire world, hence God alone is worthy of it.... A person can get sufficient guidance from natural reason and the doctrine of the Gospel," writes St. John of the Cross.[13] Although St. Teresa never formulated arguments against the anti-intellectual attitude of the Illuminists of her day, she made it clear that their ideas were abhorrent to her, if only because they went contrary to the common sense that she valued so much. Thus, she takes the position that: "Knowledge and learning are a great help in everything."[14]

The two saints are also in accord in regard to prayer. Although they strongly advocate the importance of mental prayer, in contrast to the "spirituals" of their times, they stress at every turn that the spiritual life does not consist in visions, revelations, or anything extraordinary but in the practice of solid virtue.[15] Concerning external devotions, they advocate only those of which the Church has approved. St. Teresa says: "I never cared for other devotions that some people practice, especially women, with those ceremonies intolerable to me, but to them an aid for their devotion." In another place she writes: "May God deliver us from foolish devotions."[16] St. John writes that "it would be better to convert these prayers into practices of greater importance, such as the purification of their consciences, and serious concentration upon matters pertinent to their salvation." As to vocal prayers, both agree in advising the soul to refrain from a multiplicity of words and petitions, and to use the *Pater Noster* with its seven petitions, which include "all our spiritual and temporal necessities." For in these "are embodied everything that is God's will and all that is fitting for us."[17] With these words, St. John of the Cross summarizes the famous commentary which St. Teresa writes on the same prayer in concluding the *Way of Perfection*.

Points in Which St. John Notably Supplements St. Teresa

There is not the least discrepancy between the two Carmelite Doctors as to the nature of the theological virtues, nor of their application in everyday life. St. Teresa, however, gives little attention to analyzing them, whereas St. John's treatment of these virtues surpasses in clarity and depth anything that St. Teresa has to offer.

St. John of the Cross explains that the union of the soul with God through sanctifying grace is not only conceived as it exists in the essence of the soul but also as it blossoms forth in the three faculties—intellect, memory, and will. The theological virtues that have God as their object are likewise three, one for each faculty. Faith, as it cleanses the intellect of notions that are simply human, unites the intellect to God as the First Truth. Hope, as it puts the "memory in darkness and emptiness as regards all earthly and heavenly objects," unites the soul to God as its future possession. Charity, as it withdraws affection from all that is not God, unites the will with its Beloved.[18] Therefore, in order to advance quickly in the way of union, those who are beginning to enter the state of contemplation cannot do better than devote themselves ever more intensely to practicing these virtues.

Faith frees the intellect of all imperfect knowledge of God and puts it into close contact with Him. No distinct knowledge, that is, conceptual knowledge of the intellect, can give a true idea of God's transcendent perfection. "Though truly,...all creatures carry with them a certain relationship to God...the difference which lies between His divine being and their being is infinite." Therefore, it is impossible for the intellect to be united perfectly with God by means of created things. On the other hand, faith has God in His supernatural eminence as its object. Faith believes all that God is, and so as He is three Persons in One, "it presents Him to us in this way; and as God is darkness to our intellect, so does faith dazzle and blind us." Since faith is concerned with God immediately as He is, it places the soul in direct contact with the divine object. "The more intense a man's faith, the closer is his union with God."[19]

How can this theory be applied practically to the soul which has been led into contemplation and should be led on to the divine union? In the first place, contemplation consists in a simple gaze of loving faith, enlightened by the motion of divine wisdom. Secondly, the practice of contemplation is incompatible with imaginative meditation. When God calls the soul to the state of contemplation it finds itself incapable of meditating, which often causes distress and alarm. As it progresses in contemplation, it is drawn more and more into a deeper recollection habitually devoid of distinct thoughts.[20] It may seem as though all its intellectual life is vanishing. St. John bids it not to fear. Images of meditation or distinct thoughts do not hold the mind in immediate union with God. All distinct thoughts are "as clouds which hinder a fuller communication." However, faith, loving faith, places the mind directly under the more abundant influence of the divine action.[21]

> The Holy Spirit illumines the intellect that is recollected, and He illumines it according to the mode of its recollection, and the intellect can find no better recollection than in faith, and thus the Holy Spirit will not illumine it in any other recollection more than in faith. The purer and more refined a soul is in faith, the more infused charity it possesses, and the more charity it has the more the Holy Spirit illumines it and communicates His gifts, because charity is the means by which they are communicated.[22]

Therefore, the soul that is being called to contemplation must not be frightened when it finds meditation impossible and is obliged to be content with a simple gaze of loving faith. This will unite it to God and entrust it to His sanctifying action.

As faith leads the intellect to God so hope prepares the memory for divine union. Hope renders the memory empty and brings darkness over it as to things of this life and the next; for hope is ever concerned about things not yet possessed, if they were possessed there would be no place for hope.[23] Hope makes the soul desire the possession of God and makes it look for all from Him. The more that hope takes possession of the soul, so much the less shall it desire created objects, so much the less shall it depend upon them. As these are no longer either the aspiration or the foundation upon which it builds its life, every attachment to them will vanish. Images will become less distinct and will be less of an obstacle to recollection. Hence, there is no better means of mortifying the memory than to cultivate the virtue of hope, substituting for the remembrance of precious objects, the longing to possess God, and for the support of creatures, absolute confidence in His assistance. "By Hope the soul lifts itself up to God." The virtue of hope is "an anchor which is grappled to the eternal shores where all good things come to us."[24]

Again, we must remember that St. John is "imparting instructions...for advancing in contemplation to union with God." The saint shows how contemplation itself, as it becomes deeper, envelops the soul "in great forgetfulness" of all things in order that it may be wholly occupied with God. And when it is nearing the state of union the absorption of the memory may be so great "that a person... will forget to eat or drink, or fail to remember whether or not he performed some task, or saw a particular object, or said something." However, when he attains to perfect union everything will settle into its place; he will no longer "experience these lapses of memory.... Rather he will possess greater perfection in actions" because God will rule his whole life.[25]

Faith and hope reduce the understanding and the will to a profound recollection hiding them in God. But in order to prepare them for divine union, that recollection must be loving. It is the function of charity to make it so.

God asks man, above all, for his whole heart: "You shall love the Lord, your God, with all your heart, and with all your soul, and with all your strength."[26] Nevertheless, this heart so easily becomes attached to creatures, and every attachment restricts its capacity, dissipates its strength, and renders it impossible for it to give itself wholly to God. In order to love God with a love that is deep and strong, the will must be free, utterly detached. St. John reviews all the good things of earth and presents a fundamental principle by which the heart can be kept free for the love of God: "The will should rejoice only in what is for the honor and glory of God"; anything that is not for His glory "is without value to man."[27]

There are six kinds of goods: temporal, natural, sensory, moral, supernatural, and spiritual. The first three, which refer to temporal goods can so bind the human heart that they can become occasions of offending God.[28] However, it is not impossible to make good use of them; in fact, they should even help us in going to God. St. John, himself, was highly attracted to nature, and thought of it as a positive help to devotion. His view is that God makes use of "pleasant variations in the arrangement of the land and the trees" to awaken devotion, and that such spots should be used if "one immediately directs the will to God in the forgetfulness of the place itself."[29] To such forgetfulness we owe the depth of the *Spiritual Canticle*. In the gloom of the prison of Toledo John of the Cross had pondered earnestly in his memories of a "green meadow, coated, bright with flowers," "lonely wooded valleys" and "resounding rivers"; "love-stirring breezes," tranquil nights, and the rising of the dawn. In and out of these "serene and sunny" stanzas of the *Canticle* run the three themes of woods, hills, and water in a way that leaves no doubt how frequently he recalled the scenes of the Andalusian countryside. Peers notes in his study of St. John that never is he "happier and more human, yet never more sublime, than when he writes of Nature."[30] Cristiani writes that John of the Cross "was no less enamored of the beauties of creation than was Francis of Assisi" himself.

As to music, the classical passage is also to be found in the *Spiritual Canticle*. Its being metaphorical does not dispel the impression that St. John was a genuine music-lover; anyone else would hardly have introduced the double theme of "silent music" and "sounding solitude" into a poem of pure imagination.[32] And by means of images of nature and music he lifted up his soul to sing of the beauty of his Beloved.

In the use of moral goods, such as virtues and good works, as well as extraordinary graces granted by God, there must also be great purity of intention; otherwise all their supernatural fruit may be lost by pride.[33]

Neither are spiritual goods free from dangers. It is perhaps surprising that St. John of the Cross should go so far as to discuss such aids to devotion as images, oratories, and ceremonies, all of which he seems to class as much with nature and music as with novenas and sermons. It will suffice if the saint's views on the use of images is summarized as these are identical in principle with his opinions on the rest—to forget the image and think only of what it represents:

> Images will always help a person toward union with God, provided that he does not pay more attention to them than is necessary, and that he allows himself to soar—when God bestows the favor—from the painted image to the living God, in forgetfulness of all creatures and things pertaining to creatures.[34]

Images, like nature and music, are means to an end: when they are made an end in themselves, they become dangerous.

Even in our communion with God He would not have us seek to satisfy our natural appetite for enjoyment. In a letter of spiritual direction, St. John distinguishes in the will its feeling and its act.[35] The act of the will is its love, by means of which it loves God; therefore this act is to end in God Himself. The act of the will is the real means of union with Him. The feeling, on the other hand, ends in the soul itself. It is we who feel ourselves consoled in a consolation.

There is nothing there that unites us with God. Consolation may be a means toward our loving God, provided we seize the occasion to penetrate into love. However, if we make the feeling an end we shall remain shut up in ourselves and shall not go to God. In order to love God in truth one must love Him purely, above all consolation. "With what strength will the heart be able to lift itself up to God, to plunge itself into God, which is no longer held by any bond, which is destitute of every kind of self-love! Purified by the total despoiling of itself, it will go forth to meet Him with an incredible impetus: 'with its whole strength.' "[36]

The theological virtues grow by purifying and purify by growing. To the extent that they unite us with God they empty the soul of that which is not God; and to the extent that they empty the soul of everything that is not God, the virtues unite it with God. Through the life of faith, hope, and charity, the soul uproots every ungodly thing and unites itself to God.[37]

St. John also completes St. Teresa by his teaching on asceticism. In spite of the fact that many souls are disturbed by his terminology and symbolism, this is one of the best-known features of his doctrine. The word "night," which intimidates so many persons, for St. John of the Cross means simply purification, liberation, transformation; the equivalent of the great liberation begun in baptism, by virtue of which Christians are set free from the dominion of Satan and transformed into children of God. In other words, "it is the process by which the consequences of original sin are cleared away and human nature is restored to that state of spiritual health and friendship with God which was intended at the beginning."[38]

St. John sums up his asceticism in lines which have been stumbling-blocks to many Christians:

> To reach satisfaction in all
> desire its possession in nothing.
> To come to possess all

desire the possession of nothing.
To arrive at being all
desire to be nothing.
To come to the knowledge of all
desire the knowledge of nothing.
To come to the pleasure you have not
you must go by a way in which you enjoy not.
To come to the knowledge you have not
you must go by a way in which you know not.
To come to the possession you have not
you must go by a way in which you possess not.
To come to be what you are not
you must go by a way in which you are not.[39]

In his book, *The Ascent to Truth*, Thomas Merton explains this difficult passage in the following manner:

> *Todo y Nada.* All and nothing. The two words contain the theology of St. John of the Cross. *Todo*—all—is God, who contains in Himself eminently the perfections of all things. For Him we are made. In Him we possess all things. But in order to possess Him who is all, we must renounce the possession of anything that is less than God. Every desire for knowledge, possession, being, that falls short of God must be blacked out. *Nada!*
>
> ...The key word in each of his rules for entering into the ascetic night is the word "desire." He does not say: "In order to arrive at the knowledge of everything, *know* nothing," but *"desire to know* nothing." It is not pleasure, knowledge, possession or being as such that must be "darkened" and "mortified," but only the passion of desire for these things.
>
> ...Desire, considered as a passion, is necessarily directed to a finite object. Therefore all desire imposes a *limit* to our knowledge, possessions, existence. Now, in order to escape from every limitation, we must cast off that which ties us down. There are a thousand passions which involve us in what is finite and contingent. Each one of them causes us to be occupied

with sensible things. And this occupation...narrows and closes the soul, imprisons it within its own limitations, and makes it incapable of perfect communion with the Infinite.[40]

St. John of the Cross points out at length how inordinate desires weary the soul, torment and darken it, defile and weaken it, so that it can no longer devote itself to the service of God.[41] In the whole of Book One of the *Ascent,* he explains how the soul must bring itself into conformity with Christ. In this process there is a negative aspect discarding all that is opposed to Him, and a positive one, which consists in imitating Him. In order to really appreciate this doctrine which St. John gives in this book, one must keep in mind the purpose for which he wrote. At all times he is concerned with bringing the soul to its true fulfillment which is God.

Father Crisogono makes an important comment regarding the negative aspect of St. John's doctrine:

> The *nadas* are not in the saint's mind an end but a means to be used in the beginnings of the spiritual life to avoid the danger of the inordinate affection in a heart which is still imperfect. Once purification has been effected, however, the need for this attitude ceases to exist, for the heart now purified and under control will draw good from it all. Then it not only can but must love all things, and the predilections imposed by the difference of persons and the nature of the heart—which in the saints is more genuinely human and sensitive than in others—will come to the fore, will have disappeared, while the energies for good of the passions become confirmed and strengthened.[42]

This interpretation of the *nadas* shows the contents of Book One of the *Ascent* in an encouraging light. St. John's purpose is to remove all that could prevent the soul's growth in Christ. "Austere and forbidding though his treatises may seem when we merely turn over their pages," writes E. Allison Peers, "as soon as we begin to study them in detail we find them full of serenity, beauty and under-standing."[43]

In her writings, St. Teresa does not differ from St. John in her ascetic demands but her expressions are less forceful and without paradoxes. Nonetheless, on occasion the two saints are verbally very much alike:

> It is very certain that in emptying ourselves of all that is creature and detaching ourselves from it for the love of God, the same Lord will fill us with Himself.... Fix your eyes on the Crucified and everything will become small for you.[44]

These are quotations from the writings of St. Teresa. Do they not re-echo the very words of St. John of the Cross?

Arising out of and closely connected with the question of the theological virtues and asceticism is another which concerns contemplative prayer.

In all her teaching on prayer, St. Teresa has left no definite instruction on the transition from meditation to contemplation. It is perhaps the point upon which her teaching, as a whole, is rather vague. A study which would trace out clearly the itinerary of the soul that is passing from meditative prayer to passive contemplation was the task of St. John of the Cross.

In meditation, almost everything depends upon per-sonal effort and application; in passive contemplation, the soul's cooperation may be reduced to simply receiving what God pours into it, sometimes with irresistible force. How-ever, between these two extremes there are several inter-mediate stages, in which the soul's active cooperation meets the divine infusion. In these states of mental prayer, God's working is often so delicate that it is imperceptible even to the soul receiving it. At times, the recipient of these favors opposes the operation of divine grace by a violent activity.[45]

In his works St. John particularly calls the attention of spiritual directors to the existence of these stages of prayer.[46] He has even sketched out the development in the soul of a form of mental prayer that depends, in great measure, upon its own efforts and which yet deserves the name of contemplation. It is so called either because the intellect no longer reasons but is content to gaze upon God with a simple loving attention, or because this attention is often made easier by a hidden infusion of divine light.[47]

For St. Teresa contemplation always means those degrees of prayer in which the soul experiences God's action in itself; it *feels* that it is passive. The prayer of quiet is the first degree of this contemplation.[48] In turning to St. John of the Cross, it is simply obvious that the prayer described by him in Book Two of the *Ascent* (xii-xv) and called contemplation, cannot be identified with the prayer of quiet. Referring in another place to this same prayer he calls it "the beginning of contemplation that is dark and dry to the senses...which is secret and hidden from the very one who receives it."[49] Therefore, for St. John there is a contemplation in which God *does not* make Himself felt. When he speaks of contemplation he includes lower forms of prayer than does St. Teresa, and thus uses the word "contemplation" in a wider sense than she does.[50]

A very common phenomenon prevalent in the spiritual life, known and noted by all ascetic writers, serves St. John as a point of departure for his study. At the beginning of their conversion, interior souls are usually favored with sensible spiritual sweetness, especially in the practice of meditation. However, after some time of an intense and generous spiritual life they ordinarily fall into dryness and desolation. Meditation, which was so full of delights, becomes impossible; the affections, which previously moved so easily, remain cold; instead of feeling an attraction for liturgical prayer, reception of the sacraments, practice of virtue, and works of the apostolate, they are aware of repugnance, distaste, despondency, and sadness. Formerly the soul felt itself borne up by divine grace; now it must drag itself along with every atom of strength of will. What is the meaning of all this?

Usually, spiritual writers have seen in this aridity a trial permitted or sent by God, in order to test the soul's fidelity. St. John certainly does not differ from them in this opinion, but he has greatly enriched this common teaching. He has shown more clearly how this testing is necessary for the soul, and that it is God Himself who, by His infusion, causes this aridity, in order to raise the soul to a higher and more profitable state of prayer.[51]

Because it is so difficult to free oneself entirely from all self-love, God comes with His assistance by plunging the soul into the bitterness of the passive night of the senses. How could He fail to help anyone who is generous, if it be true, as St. John says, that "if a person is seeking God," much more is God seeking Him.[52]

Normally God Himself comes to place the soul in aridity, in order to free it from its too great subjection to the life of the senses, and makes it live more spiritually. St. John gives three signs by which the soul can be assured that the aridity is really brought about by God Himself and not by its own infidelity, tepidity, or physical indisposition.[53]

The first sign consists in a disinclination to occupy oneself not only with God but also with creatures. Since the soul has renounced all affection for creatures and does not concern itself with them, the first common cause of aridity is ruled out: unfaithfulness, the sins committed which always leave in the soul some inclination towards creatures. The second sign is a certain anxiety by which the soul becomes imbued with the idea that perhaps "it is not serving God but turning back, because it is aware of this distaste for the things of God." By this it is plain that the aridity does not proceed from lukewarmness. Lukewarm souls do not trouble themselves about the service of God.

The third sign is the actual inability to meditate, which continues to increase, thus showing that it is not caused by bodily indisposition, which is ordinarily passing.[54] The soul that recognizes these signs in itself should feel comforted, for this aridity shows that it is being called to contemplation. It is God Himself who, with the help of His infused light, comes to second the soul's own effort in bringing about the transition from meditation to contemplation. Therefore, let it "trust in God who does not fail those who seek Him with a simple and righteous heart," and "since He is the supernatural artificer, He will construct supernaturally in each soul the edifice He desires."[55]

St. John then goes on to give direction to fervent souls that fall into dryness through no fault of their own. On no account will he have them forced to meditate. He declares expressly that the time for meditation is passed and:

> they should allow the soul to remain in rest and quietude, even though it may seem very obvious to them that they are doing nothing and wasting time, and even though they think this disinclination to think about anything is due to their laxity. Through patience and perseverance in prayer, they will be doing a great deal without activity on their part. All that is required of them here is freedom of soul, that they liberate themselves from the impediment and fatigue of ideas and thoughts and care not about thinking and meditating. They must be content simply with a loving and peaceful attentiveness to God, and live without the concern, without the effort, and without the desire to taste or feel Him. All these desires disquiet the soul and distract it from the peaceful quiet and sweet idleness of the contemplation which is being communicated to it.[56]

The detachment engendered through the theological virtues should preserve peacefulness of soul without which there can be no progress in contemplation. For, as St. John says, "this contemplation is active while the soul is in idleness and unconcern. It is like air that escapes when one tries to grasp it in one's hands."[57]

Consequently, there is a notable difference psychologically between the soul that receives the infused light in a hidden manner and the one that enjoys it experientially. The latter *feels* "the love with which He is drawing it nearer to Himself," and its whole occupation must consist in carefully cherishing this love. Therefore, as St. Teresa teaches, it must not allow its intellect to investigate what is happening within it; rather it must remain still and follow the movement which it feels comes to its will from God Himself.[58]

On the other hand, the soul that *feels nothing* of this divine action must be made aware that God is really working within it. But it needs special guidance to enable it to identify the hidden operation which has begun. Because this divine action is very delicate, it must learn not only how not to hinder it, but also how to *maintain itself* in the best disposition for receiving it; and this instruction it ought to receive from its spiritual director.[59] "If there is no one to understand these persons, they either turn back and abandon the road or lose courage, or at least they hinder their own progress."[60]

St. John of the Cross, Doctor of the Universal Church, has delineated certain signs when the soul should abandon ordinary, discursive meditation in order to occupy itself completely in remaining intent upon God in loving faith. He logically makes the three signs "an integral part of his grand synthesis of the evolution of the contemplative life, giving them their full significance and explaining their importance."[61] These signs which "have become classic in the study of spiritual theology," are meant to bring great comfort to the soul that observes them in its case.[62] Instead of being miserable because it has fallen into dryness, and fearing that it has gone back, it has every reason to be thankful. God has come to free it from the yoke of the senses, under which it was kept of necessity by meditation, in order to transfer it to a more spiritual state of prayer. And now it will be able to reach "a deeper intimacy with God and will see infinite horizons opening out before it for the future." Under one condition, however: that it learns to be content with simply "beholding Him in loving faith."[63]

With this, his luminous doctrine, St. John of the Cross becomes the great consoler of troubled souls. In this way the "Doctor of the Dark Night" supplements the teaching of St. Teresa on contemplation.

Points in Which St. Teresa Notably Supplements St. John

While the treatises of St. John of the Cross are distinguished for their "profundity and a clear grasp of essential principles," St. Teresa's writings are characterized by their "brilliance, the accuracy of their descriptions, and the down-to-earth quality of her advice," especially to beginners in the spiritual life. For them, she shows a truly motherly sympathy and insight. If there were no introduction to the way of perfection beyond the stern principles of St. John, many might never be induced to begin. The writings of St. Teresa fill this "real need."[64]

St. Teresa treats of beginners in her descriptions of the first water in her *Life*, Dwelling Places I, II, and III in the *Interior Castle*, and in the greater part of the *Way of Perfection*. She is full of loving solicitude for the beginners in her instructions. "In the beginning," she writes, strive "to walk in joy and freedom." She tells them to recreate "so as to be able to return with greater strength to prayer." Knowing how difficult beginners find the practice of virtue, she prods them on with words of encouragement. For those who cannot meditate, she offers alternatives. She holds out high ideals and tells them not to be afraid to aspire to them for "His Majesty wants this determination, and He is a friend of courageous souls if they walk in humility and without trusting in self."[65] Although she is not discouraged by failures, neither is she overly indulgent with weakness. When her counsels to beginners are analyzed they are just as stern as those of St. John, but she knows how to present them in a manner more acceptable to human nature. Her deep spiritual wisdom and common sense were "purchased dearly, at a cost of many errors, initial carelessness, and faulty direction, all of which God turned to good use for herself and for many others."[66]

Since St. Teresa had already fulfilled the needs of beginners, there was no need for St. John to concentrate on them. He does not lack understanding or care for those starting out on the road to perfection, but he is chiefly concerned with guiding souls in the transitional period from meditation to contemplation. He realizes that so many go astray or turn back when they reach this stage in the spiritual life. He is also fully aware of the fact that while many practice meditation, there are relatively few who practice the virtues which should accompany it. For this reason he gives more attention to detachment than to the early stages of prayer.

Affective spirituality is another point of which Saint Teresa treats at considerable length, whereas St. John of the Cross gives it only a passing reference. His main concern is the cultivation of the theological virtues. The infused joys of affective prayer for him are only "stepping-stone(s) to true interior perfection." However, a large portion of the Church's literature, especially the Franciscan school which is principally derived from St. Bonaventure, deals with the affective aspect of the spiritual life. The influence of its contemporary representatives, Francisco de Osuna and Bernadino de Laredo, can be detected in the writings of St. Teresa. She "regarded the infused delights which souls are liable to experience in the prayer of the will as a valuable preparation" and "a source of encouragement in the time of trial."[67] However, reflecting on her own experience she writes that because she was excessively attached to these consolations much time was lost and strength exhausted profiting her soul very little. Therefore, she constantly urges humility and detachment to sensible graces.[68]

Although St. John devotes little space to analyzing affective prayer, he is even more emphatic than St. Teresa in cautioning the soul of attachment to the joys which may come with it. He agrees with St. Teresa that "God gives us these gifts" for which we should "be grateful to His Majesty," but there is a certain dissonance that can be detected in the practical advice they give.[69] St. John writes that "It is always good for man to reject them with closed eyes.... Faith alone...should be the light we use" on our spiritual journey.[70] Although St. Teresa admits that it would be more perfect to do without favors, she shows a certain partiality for them. "Others," she says, "may find they have need of no more than the truth of faith in order to perform very perfect works—and I, being so miserable, have had need of everything."[71]

With regard to the Humanity of Christ there are those who claim that the doctrine of St. Teresa is irreconcilable with that of St. John's doctrine. St. Teresa insists that it is never right to deprive the understanding of the remembrance of Jesus Christ, whereas St. John is constantly advocating attention to God in pure faith, devoid of every image, even that of the sacred Humanity.[72]

The truth is that St. Teresa refers her criticism to those who are voluntarily putting away every thought of our Lord because they consider such a remembrance an obstacle to the progress of contemplation. On the other hand, Saint John of the Cross speaks of a soul that finds it impossible to meditate and form distinct concepts, such as that of the sacred Humanity. These are two perfectly distinct situations. St. John instructs the soul to be content with focusing its attention upon God in a general way, without forcing itself to form concepts when God renders it incapable of meditation. Nevertheless, when it should perceive that it is not remaining in contact with God, it must return to meditation and distinct concepts, where at once, it will find the remembrance of Christ. St. John speaks directly to those "who have begun to enter the state of contemplation."[73] It would be a mistake to apply the instruction given to contemplatives to those who are still in need of meditation. For the latter, the reflection upon the life and Passion of our Lord should be the "daily food" of their mental prayer.[74]

However, St. Teresa deals explicitly with one question which St. John touches only implicitly, that is, the place which the sacred Humanity must hold in contemplative prayer. She first refers to this theme in her *Life,* where she refutes in vigorous terms the teaching of those who would exclude our Lord's Humanity from contemplation.[75] The spiritual writers of the time, including Francisco de Osuna, advocated this practice.[76] For some years, St. Teresa herself had accepted their teaching by "not delighting so much in the thought of our Lord Jesus Christ but in going along in that absorption, waiting for that enjoyment." But very soon she saw clearly that she "was proceeding badly."[77] Although this error was but transient, it left her with sharp regrets:

> At no time do I recall this opinion I had without feeling pain; it seems to me I became a dreadful traitor—although in ignorance. ...Is it possible, my Lord, that it entered my mind for even an hour that You would be an impediment to my greater good?[78]

By her vigorous discussion of the dangerous assertions of those masters who were leading her astray, she proves her doctrine; namely, that "in all the states of the spiritual life one must return to the Humanity of our Lord and never withdraw from it as long as grace does not lead us elsewhere."[79] This is one of the clearest instances of how St. Teresa of Jesus completes St. John of the Cross.

Alleged Contradictions Between
St. Teresa and St. John

Though writing from different standpoints with a common end, there are no open contradictions, but possibly some grounds for alleged differences. One is their teaching on apostolic activity, and the other has to do with visions and revelations.

Among the many passages from the writings of St. Teresa which seem to show her unqualified zeal for the active life, is the following taken from the *Foundations:*

> It is here, my daughters, that love is to be found—not hidden away in corners but in the midst of occasions of sin; and believe me, although we may more often fail and commit more lapses, our gain will be incomparably the greater.... It would be a bad business if we could practice prayer only by getting alone in corners.[80]

On the other hand, a citation from her *Life* portrays the opposite.

> The most we have to strive for in the beginning is to care for oneself alone and consider that there is nothing on earth but God and oneself—and this practice is very beneficial.[81]

Like St. Teresa, St. John proves to be a no less unqualified advocate of solitude and contemplation. In the *Spiritual Canticle* he clearly writes:

> Once the soul reaches this state of union of love...she should not become involved in other works and exterior exercises that might be of the slightest hindrance to the attentiveness of love toward God, even though the work be of great service to God. For a little of this pure love is more precious to God and the soul and more beneficial to the Church, even though it seems one is doing nothing, than all these other works put together.[82]

However, his "Spiritual Sayings" cite proof of a counter-position, also.

> The supreme perfection of souls in their rank and degree is to progress and grow, according to their talent and means, in the imitation of God, and the most wondrous and divine thing is to be a cooperator with Him in the conversion and conquest of souls.[83]

As a solution to this seeming dilemma, one needs to understand the two tendencies in supernatural charity as it is found among those here on earth. Where one seeks to work in the apostolate of souls, the other longs to bury itself in God. Yet each is a movement of divine love, and each finds its perfect synthesis in complete conformity with Christ. Following the impulse of grace and the commands of obedience, the soul is free to express itself in either way at different times.

As St. John points out in his *Canticle,* "pure love" depends on God's will and is always of immense value to the Church. For some souls, the call is to apostolic work animated by love, and for others, it is a call to literal solitude. In either calling, the soul begins to realize as it advances in union with its Spouse, that the ultimate perfection cannot be attained until it identifies itself with the works of Redemption. Whatever the soul does, depends entirely on God's will and its own possession of sanctifying grace and the theological virtues, which make possible the indwelling of God in the soul, and His full possession of it as an effective instrument.[84]

Of the numerous asserted contradictions between St. Teresa and St. John, none has attracted more attention perhaps than their attitude toward visions, locutions, and other mystical phenomena. Where St. Teresa attaches considerable importance to them and encourages the soul to enjoy them, St. John rejects them. However oversimplified as this may be, the true position is almost exactly parallel to that of "infused joys" which have previously been described.[85]

It is true to say that St. Teresa valued supernatural favors and was grateful to God for them. In the *Life* and *Relations* she attributes much of her own spiritual progress to visions of our Lord, and even in the *Interior Castle,* she speaks of the good that can be effected by them, especially when they concern our Lord's Humanity. But she is adamant that before accepting them, one must first of all, be certain that they come from God and are not a freak of the imagination, or one of the devil's wiles. Therefore, she cautions souls that they should always communicate this to a competent and learned director.[86] Having experienced the high price that has to be paid for such favors, she constantly warns them not to expect any of these favors, still less to desire them. For "when there is a great desire," the imagination "makes a person think that he sees what he desires and hears it." Although St. Teresa realizes that these favors may be very helpful, she admits that they are not necessary to perfection: "...there are many holy persons who have never received one of these favors; and others who receive them but are not holy."[87]

Where St. Teresa sometimes speaks in praise of them, St. John of the Cross only recognizes extraordinary favors as a means by which "God is leading" certain souls.[88] He insists that "a person should be careful never to accept them—unless in some rare cases and with extremely competent advice, and then without any desire for them." For if favors are genuine, "they produce their main effect in the soul passively," independently of any cooperation from the recipient, thus safeguarding against delusion and pride.[89] In view of the particular purpose for which he is writing, he says that because these favors are limited and particular, they can never "serve as a means for union since they bear no proportion to God."[90]

In the *Spiritual Canticle,* St. John presents an example of a practical application of his theory on extraordinary favors. He says that the bride-soul has four desires: "First, that He be pleased to communicate Himself to her very inwardly, in the hiding place of the soul." This means that she aspires to transforming union through faith and the gifts of the Holy Spirit, not to accidental phenomena such as visions and revelations. "Second, that He inform and shine upon her faculties with the glory and excellence of His divinity"; nothing less can satisfy her. "Third, that this communication be so sublime and profound that she may neither desire nor know how to give a description of it, and that the sensory and exterior part be incapable of receiving it." By this is meant essentially union, unalloyed by sensible phenomena. "Fourth, that He be enamored of the virtues and graces" that He Himself has placed in her, enabling her to soar aloft to God by means of a high and noble knowledge of the Divinity. In this passage St. John brings out clearly that such phenomena should not be sought since they are unnecessary for arriving at full union with God. However, he does not outrightly reject them but gives a recommendation to his readers to consult the writings of St. Teresa, who, he says: "left writings about these spiritual matters, which are admirably done and which I hope will soon be printed and brought to light."[91]

This alleged antithesis between the two saints concerning extraordinary favors is probably a question of emphasis. In any event both agree that such phenomena are only secondary since they cease entirely once the soul reaches the stage of spiritual marriage.[92] Where St. Teresa permits one to rejoice in them under certain conditions, because their worth is questionable, St. John says that it is better not to rejoice in them at all. No matter how one views the question, one who has read the writings of the two Carmelite saints cannot but be impressed by their "sane attitude to the extraordinary element in the spiritual life, an attitude opposed both to the credulity and scepticism which are so common in our age."[93]

In studying the works of these two Mystical Doctors in conjunction with each other, there is much evidence of contrasts, comparisons, and similarities. Where St. Teresa could not have reached the heights of spiritual wisdom and maturity without St. John, he on the other hand, needed her to introduce him to the world, "for at first sight he gives the impression of being aloof from reality." Together their writings enshrine the riches of a spiritual heritage for all the people of God who are seeking "to live even here on earth a heavenly life" by sharing this life with one another in anticipation of unending glory.[94]

FOOTNOTES

1. *Ascent,* I, i, 2; ii, 1; Kavanaugh-Rodriguez, 73-75.
2. *Ascent,* I, xiii, 3; Kavanaugh-Rodriguez, 102.
3. *Ascent,* II, vi, 8; Kavanaugh-Rodriguez, 121.
4. *Ascent,* II, v, 3; Kavanaugh-Rodriguez, 116.
5. Kavanaugh, Introduction to the *Spiritual Canticle,* 399.
6. *Spiritual Canticle,* XII, 3; Kavanaugh-Rodriguez, 499.
7. *Ascent,* II, v, 3; Kavanaugh-Rodriguez, 116.
8. *Living Flame,* I, 15; Kavanaugh-Rodriguez, 585.
9. Father Gabriel, O.D.C., "St. Teresa of Jesus and St. John of the Cross," *St. Teresa of Avila: Studies in Her Life, Doctrine and Times* (Dublin: Clonmore and Reynolds, Ltd., 1963), 46-47. Reprinted with permission of Search Press, Ltd., London.
10. *Ibid.,* 47-48.
11. *Ibid.*
12. *Way of Perfection,* 17; Kavanaugh-Rodriguez, II, 99.
13. "Sayings of Light and Love," 32; *Ascent,* II, xxi, 4; Kavanaugh-Rodriguez, 670, 174.
14. *Interior Castle,* IV, 1; Kavanaugh-Rodriguez, II, 318.
15. *Interior Castle,* VI, 6; VII, 4; Kavanaugh-Rodriguez, II, 392, 447.
16. *Life,* 6, 13; Kavanaugh-Rodriguez, I, 53, 94.
17. *Ascent,* III, xliv, 1, 4; Kavanaugh-Rodriguez, 288-289.
18. *Ascent,* II, vi, 1, 3, 4; Kavanaugh-Rodriguez, 119-120.
19. *Ascent,* II, viii, 3; ix, 1; Kavanaugh-Rodriguez, 126, 129.
20. *Ascent,* II, xiii, 1-2; xiv, 10; Kavanaugh-Rodriguez, 140, 145-146.
21. Father Gabriel of St. Mary Magdalen, *St. John of the Cross: Doctor of Divine Love and Contemplation,* trans. by a Benedictine of Stanbrook Abbey (Cork: The Mercier Press, 1947), 33-35.

22. Ascent, II, xxix, 6; Kavanaugh-Rodriguez, 205.

23. Ascent, II, vi, 3; Kavanaugh-Rodriguez, 119.

24. Gabriel of St. Mary Magdalen, St. John of the Cross, 38.

25. Ascent, III, ii, 2, 4, 8; Kavanaugh-Rodriguez, 214-216.

26. Dt. 6:5; Ascent, III, xvii, 2; Kavanaugh-Rodriguez, 239.

27. Ascent, III, xvii, 2; Kavanaugh-Rodriguez, 239.

28. Ascent, III, xvii, 2; xviii, 1; Kavanaugh-Rodriguez, 239-240.

29. Ascent, III, xlii, i; Kavanaugh-Rodriguez, 285.

30. E. Allison Peers, Spirit of Flame: A Study of St. John of the Cross (New York: Morehouse-Gorman Co., 1945), 194-195.

31. Leon Cristiani, St. John of the Cross: Prince of Mystical Theology, trans. from the French (Garden City, N.Y.: Doubleday & Company, Inc., 1962), 231.

32. Peers, Spirit of Flame, 195.

33. Ascent, III, xxvii-xxxi; Kavanaugh-Rodriguez, 260-270.

34. Ascent, III, xv, 2; Kavanaugh-Rodriguez, 237.

35. Letter, XII; Kavanaugh-Rodriguez, 692-695.

36. Gabriel of St. Mary Magdalen, St. John of the Cross, 41-42.

37. Kavanaugh, Introduction to the Ascent, 53.

38. Gabriel, "St. Teresa and St. John," 53-54.

39. Ascent, I, xiii, 11; Kavanaugh-Rodriguez, 103-104.

40. Thomas Merton, The Ascent to Truth, 53-54. Copyright 1951 by The Abbey of Our Lady of Gethsemani; renewed 1979 by The Merton Legacy Trust. Reprinted by permission of Harcourt, Brace, Jovanovich, Inc.

41. Ascent, I, vi, 1; Kavanaugh-Rodriguez, 84ff.

42. Crisogono de Jesus, O.C.D., The Life of St. John of the Cross, trans. by Kathleen Pond (New York: Harper and Brothers, 1958), 311.

43. Peers, Spirit of Flame, 198.

44. Interior Castle, VII, 2, 4; Kavanaugh-Rodriguez, II, 435-436, 446.

45. Gabriel of St. Mary Magdalen, St. John of the Cross, 100.

46. Living Flame, III, 30; Kavanaugh-Rodriguez, 621ff.

47. Gabriel of St. Mary Magdalen, St. John of the Cross, 101.

48. Interior Castle, IV, 1; Kavanaugh-Rodriguez, II, 316.

49. Dark Night, I, ix, 6; Kavanaugh-Rodriguez, 315.

50. Gabriel of St. Mary Magdalen, St. John of the Cross, 112-113.

51. Ibid., 47-48.

52. Living Flame, III, 28; Kavanaugh-Rodriguez, 620.

53. Dark Night, I, ix, 1; Kavanaugh-Rodriguez, 313.

54. Dark Night, I, ix, 2, 3, 9; Kavanaugh-Rodriguez, 313-316.

55. Dark Night, I, x, 3; Living Flame, III, 47; Kavanaugh-Rodriguez, 317, 628.

56. Dark Night, I, x, 4; Kavanaugh-Rodriguez, 317.

57. Dark Night, I, ix, 6; Kavanaugh-Rodriguez, 315.

58. Interior Castle, IV, 2; Life, 15; Kavanaugh-Rodriguez, II, 325; I, 104.

59. Gabriel of St. Mary Magdalen, St. John of the Cross, 121-122.

60. Dark Night, I, 10; Kavanaugh-Rodriguez, 317.

61. Gabriel of St. Mary Magdalen, St. John of the Cross, 148.

62. Father Kieran, O.C.D., "St. John of the Cross: On Aridity and Contemplation," Spiritual Life, viii (Fall, 1962), 184.

63. Gabriel of St. Mary Magdalen, St. John of the Cross, 149.

64. Gabriel, "St. Teresa and St. John," 58-59.

65. Life, 13; Kavanaugh-Rodriguez, I, 89.

66. Gabriel, "St. Teresa and St. John," 59-60.
67. *Ibid.*
68. *Interior Castle*, IV, 3; Kavanaugh-Rodriguez, II, 326-327.
69. *Ascent*, III, xvi-xlv; Kavanaugh-Rodriguez, 237-292; *Life*, x; Peers, I, 59.
70. *Ascent*, II, xi, 8; xvi, 15; Kavanaugh-Rodriguez, 134-135, 155.
71. *Life*, 10; Kavanaugh-Rodriguez, I, 76.
72. Gabriel, "St. Teresa and St. John," 63.
73. *Ascent*, II, vi, 8; Kavanaugh-Rodriguez, 121.
74. Gabriel of St. Mary Magdalen, *St. John of the Cross*, 173.
75. *Life*, 22; Kavanaugh-Rodriguez, I, 144.
76. P. Marie-Eugene, *I Want to See God*, 68.
77. *Interior Castle*, VI, 7; Kavanaugh-Rodriguez, II, 404.
78. *Life*, 22; Kavanaugh-Rodriguez, I, 145.
79. P. Marie Eugene, *I Want to See God*, 68.
80. *Foundations*, V; Peers, III, 25.
81. *Life*, 13; Kavanaugh-Rodriguez, I, 92.
82. *Spiritual Canticle*, XXIX, 2; Kavanaugh-Rodriguez, 523.
83. St. John of the Cross, "Spiritual Sayings," *The Complete Works of Saint John of the Cross: Doctor of the Church,* Vol. III, trans. and edited by E. Allison Peers (Westminster, Md: Newman Press, 1953), 292. Reprinted with permission of Search Press, Ltd., London.
84. Gabriel, "St. Teresa and St. John," 66-67.
85. Above, 87-88.
86. *Life*, 23; Kavanaugh-Rodriguez, I, 152-154.
87. *Interior Castle*, VI, 9; Kavanaugh-Rodriguez, II, 416-417.
88. *Ascent*, II, xxii, 19; xvii, 4; Kavanaugh-Rodriguez, 186, 156.
89. *Ascent*, II, xi, 13; xvi, 10; Kavanaugh-Rodriguez, 136, 153.
90. *Ascent*, II, xi, 12; Kavanaugh-Rodriguez, 136.
91. *Spiritual Canticle*, XIX, 2; XIII, 7; Kavanaugh-Rodriguez, 486, 460.
92. *Interior Castle*, VII, 3; Kavanaugh-Rodriguez, II, 442; *Dark Night*, II, i, 2; Kavanaugh-Rodriguez, 330-331.
93. Gabriel, "St. Teresa and St. John," 69.
94. *Ibid.*, 70-71.

5. The Implications of Teresian Spiritual Theology in the Contemporary World

Contemporary Hunger for Mysticism

One of the more striking spiritual developments of the recent past is a new craving for religious experience. Having sprung up suddenly, it is beginning to flourish in the face of the apathetic attitude that prevails toward religious matters in the Western world. This ferment frequently seems to occur in people who have abandoned churches and formal religion. Some are consciously seeking a personal encounter with God, while others do not fully comprehend that the experience they seek is essentially religious. Likewise, the same thirst is manifested more moderately and negatively in those who refuse to attend church services because they do not find them "meaningful" and "relevant."[1]

It is becoming more and more obvious that our society and culture have had too little of the mystical. Hence, for a long time creative people have given their critique of the vacuum in our modern culture. In the twenties, T. S. Eliot already imaged the shallowness of modern life in "The Hallow Men." In the same year F. Scott Fitzgerald wrote *The Great Gatsby,* blaming that emptiness in the American way of life on man's inability to be contemplative, and on his inability to wonder. More than ever before man is especially conscious of the lack of the mystical qualities in our culture.[2]

Especially the young hunger for these qualities with the result that some have turned to the occult and many to psychedelic drugs. Hundreds of young Americans with shaven heads and saffron robes chant the praises of Hare Krishna on the streets of our cities. There are even groups calling themselves "Jesus Freaks," ex-hippies, once freaking out on drugs and acid, now proclaiming that the true experience is the experience of Jesus. Others who are seeking a path to "meaning" in life, searching for contact with God, are turning to the East for guidance, inspiration and help. And within the framework of the established churches, those whose needs of security and emotion were being met inadequately or not at all, have adopted the Pentecostal spirituality.

The Pseudo-Mysticism of the Occult

In a scientific age, why do hundreds of daily newspapers print a syndicated horoscope? Does anyone really believe that the location of the stars on the day of one's birth determines his destiny? Apparently some do. With all that is now known of psychology and sociology, why believe in demonology and witchcraft? Why do otherwise intelligent modern Americans appear to believe in voodoo charms, locks of hair, candles, beads, flowers, lotions and potions, to ward off danger and ensure good luck?[3]

In her book on mysticism Georgia Harkness poses the above questions and attempts to answer them by saying that some people regard such acts and objects to be symbols of unseen powers which may possibly be related to God. However, this points to the fact that even in a scientific and technological age, science does not have all the answers to life. Though mysticism and astrology agree on this point, it cannot be concluded that astrology is mysticism.[4]

Possibly, some persons may become involved in false mysticism because of the painful discipline called for by the truer forms. Others again may yield to superstition because of an unrealistic adherence to outmoded customs or preoccupations resulting from a sick mind. Also the widespread literature of occultism and superstition which is eagerly accepted by the lettered and unlettered alike is another reason for today's interest.[5] The disappearance of genuine religion and the worldwide sweep of a materialistic attitude to life is still another reason for the flood of superstition in our times.

According to the findings of ethnologists and scholars of comparative religion, the rise of magic and superstition among civilized peoples throughout the ages is an indication of gradual religious decay. The basic law of comparative religion, that superstition is a product of disintegration and a shading of 'the original religious attitude of the nations, remains true of modern man. Whenever man strays from the pure path of belief, or when he squelches the inner longing and hunger in his soul for eternity and God, the religious emotions flee elsewhere to take refuge in the realism of the grossest superstition.[6]

Tertullian asserts that the human soul is drawn by her need to depend on and to revere the highest good; so it naturally turns toward Christianity. Being that this feeling cannot be stifled, it is possible that it can be unconsciously misdirected to express itself through offshoots of superstition.[7]

Catholic teaching clarifies the essence of superstition as a deification of the creature, as it transfers, contrary to reason, the divine attributes to a created thing. It dishonors the Creator and Lord of the world, which as such, is a sin against the virtue of divine worship.[8] Through the years the

Church has appreciated the basic human need for tangible things of sense in relating to God and things divine, as well as the possibility that it will sometimes seek expression in unreasonable practices. Despite Christ's provision of the sacramental system, some of the more usual symptoms of typical superstition are:

> fascination of the primitive, illogical reasoning, a false conception of the powers of nature, a blind obsession with the sinister powers of fate, a fear of ungodly forces that threaten one's life, and an antisocial and egotistical attitude that leads one to view commonly accepted practices of religion as inadequate.[9]

Hence what St. Paul said in his day concerning heathen idolatry is still true today of modern superstition:

> They certainly had knowledge of God, yet they did not glorify him as God or give him thanks; they stultified themselves through speculating to no purpose, and their senseless hearts were darkened. They claimed to be wise, but turned into fools instead (Rom. 1:21-22).

Likewise, the experience of all ages has been and continues to be the same—wherever faith begins to fade away there superstition will grow profusely.

Mystical Experience by Way of Drugs

The current trend toward the easy pseudo-mysticism of psychedelic drugs dates back centuries to the people of India. "It is no secret that these drugs do produce psychedelic visions and experiences—even certain powers."[10] At home, too, in the American Southwest the button-like tops of the mescal cactus, or peyote, were chewed by the Indians in their religious ceremonies, and the mescaline of today is in continuity with this practice.

As long ago as 1874, Benjamin Blood began to promote what he called "the anaesthetic revelation," claiming a gained insight into "the genius of being" by experimentation with "nitrous oxide and ether."[11] This further aroused the interest of William James, and prompted him to try some experiments himself. In the *Varieties of Religious Experiences,* the latter indicates the possibility of inducing by drugs something very similar to a mystical experience, but without giving it full endorsement.[12]

However, this major inducement to "consciousness-changing" through drugs lies much closer to our own day. In the early 1960's Timothy Leary, an instructor of clinical psychology at Harvard, promoted the use of LSD, not only as a consciousness-hanging drug in times of boredom or other malaise but as having religious significance. His formula, "Turn on. Tune in. Drop out," became a familiar password. Psychedelic experiments were set up, in which Alan Watts, a major participant, gave the next major impetus in the direction of psychedelic mysticism tinged with a bit of Zen, by means of his *Joyous Cosmology* which appeared in 1962.

With an increased consumption of drugs in the sixties, with and more often without a religious significance, the drug problem reached the alarming proportions of today. It is a desperately serious social issue. As to its mystical consciousness, it can hardly be regarded as a true form of mystical experience. Instead of dedicating one's body and mind to the service of God with all one's powers, such a drug-induced "trip," even with a religious aura, burns the body with chemicals in the hope of inducing an ecstatic sensation. Besides, the motive is selfish. Although the mystics of the classical tradition often sought inner peace rather than large-scale societal changes, they virtually always sought to relieve the suffering of others in their immediate situation. The quest for the Beatific Vision through self-renunciation has had a very different motivation from the drug-induced type. The latter seeks a pleasurable feeling whereas true mysticism centers in God. The after-effects are also quite different. Drugs leave a hangover by a disturbing effect on the brain; somewhat similar to the effect of alcohol, whereas the practice of the presence of God leaves one prepared for the service of God with a new sense of divinely given energy and strength.[13]

According to Thomas Merton's comment on the easy pseudo-mysticism of psychedelic drugs, "the appetite for experiences—or, more crudely, for kicks—is one of the greatest dangers to the development of an authentic mystical life."[14]

Kavanaugh claims that the psychedelic drug cannot produce a supernatural mystical experience, for this is God's gift to man. If, in rare cases, it can produce something identical to a natural mystical experience, this would have to be demonstrated. However, this would be a most difficult undertaking. Today, as always, the devout Christian has no need of an LSD experience in his journey to union with God. Rather he should walk steadfastly in the path of pure faith and love and poverty of spirit. "How happy are the poor in spirit; theirs is the kingdom of heaven." In walking along this path he disposes himself to receive but does not ever produce the mystical experience. This gift is granted only when God wishes to bestow His favor.[15]

Hare Krishna Consciousness

Because today's younger generation tended to reject organized churchgoing and yet was searching for fulfillment in some form of mysticism, a new cult arose within the contemporary American society.

This new cult, the Hare Krishna Movement, is a legacy from Indian religion and finds its main source in the Bhagavad Gita and the worship of Krishna as the incarnation of God. Their Bible is Gita, and their Christ is Krishna.

Hare Krishna is substantially a direct protest against the Establishment, the churches, and the Christian faith in which many of its disciples were reared. These devotees who have turned away either from Christianity, Islam or Judaism have lost faith with the personal God of these religions and are looking for a mystical religion without absolutes. These people in the Krishna Movement have turned to Hinduism, a cult that is highly personalistic. Since they accept a personal god, they transferred some of their Christian background to a Hindu sect.[16]

On the busy downtown streets or at elevated train stations, a group of these young Americans in saffron robes can be heard chanting praises to Hare Krishna. These chants are nothing like the silent prayers usually associated with mystical meditation. Yet praises are chanted to "clear the dust from one's soul, banish the *maya* which separates one from God, and bring the chanter into closer relation with God by invoking Krishna and thus evoking the Krishna Consciousness.[17]

By means of this movement, these young adults have come to realize their new identities. Having given up the habits of taking drugs, indulging in illicit sex, and drinking alcohol, they have taken on a new moral code. In a close bond of social unity, they respond as a coherent group with a common purpose of worshiping Krishna, the god unknown to them before becoming involved in this movement.

Yoga

It is a sign of our times that more and more people in the West are being attracted to the various forms of Oriental mysticism and asceticism. Articles on Yoga frequently appear in newspapers and general interest magazines, while paperbacks abound. Its popular appeal is basically a system of efficacious physical culture, with much emphasis on weight control and beauty of figure. However, those who do not go beyond this point of Yoga are practitioners of Hatha Yoga, using the techniques for hygienic or display reasons alone. This American popularization of Hatha Yoga as merely a system of physical culture, is altogether misleading. For as a way of life, Yoga has its roots in pre-historic India. It is also one of the six important Indian philosophical systems as well as a spiritual technique.[18]

From the very beginning of Indian culture, Yoga came to be considered a means of controlling the senses and the mind to attain a state of mystical union with the Divine Being, and a liberation from the ever-circling wheel of life. The two elements of magic and mysticism have always been closely interwoven in Yoga. On the one hand it is regarded as means of acquiring preternatural powers; but on the other, it is a means of liberating the soul from the bondage of matter and restoring it to its original state as a pure spirit.[19]

Based on the doctrine of the Samkhya school of philosophy, Classical Yoga believes that the soul is by nature a pure spirit that has become identified through ignorance with matter. Its purpose is to set the soul free by a conscious and unconscious technique of control of body and mind, until the mind reaches the state of "concentration on a single point" in which it is no longer subject to the influence of the body.[20]

Mircea Eliade points out that in all the forms of Yoga there is a constant effort to return to the state of man before the Fall in order to transcend the human state and become "like God." Relying on human effort and a definite technique to attain this end, Yoga may be regarded as a system of magic, and undoubtedly this element is often present. Following the original impulse of the Indian mind in its search for God, however, there is definitely a desire to attain to spiritual freedom, to be freed of the effects of sin, and frequently to depend on the grace of God rather than on human effort. In the latter case, the goal is not so much magical as mystical. Here the aim is a separation of the soul from its subjection to the body and its passions, a freedom of the mind from its subjection to the senses and the imagination, and the attainment to a state of absolute freedom and spiritual consciousness. Hence, it is believed that man can be restored to his original state of unity beyond the flux of time and change. By a freedom from the bondage to the material world, man can be established in immortality. This absolute freedom marks the deep aspiration of the Indian soul to recover the lost state of Paradise and to return to God. Lacking the light of revelation, it is undoubtedly exposed to the dangers of magical and superstitious illusions. Yet, on the whole, the fundamental motive of Yoga is still a sincere desire to be united with God.[21]

"Nervous, highly strung or elderly persons are advised not to take up Yoga. The breathing and postural exercises that are normally soothing would only increase their tensions and tire them out."[22] Also, advanced stages of Yoga or the popularized candle meditation could become quite harmful without expert guidance.[23]

Zen Buddhism

Recently, writings about Zen and its possible introduction into Christianity have evolved in the field of spiritual classics. At its deepest level Zen has been handed down from master to disciple from the time of Bodhidharma, the legendary founder of Chinese Zen. It is a process of unification in which the whole personality is integrated into a oneness which reaches its climax in *satori* or enlightenment. The famous lotus position of Zen, which can be learned from books, is only a means of an interior attitude of mind and heart which is reached mainly by detachment. This Oriental detachment includes a technique for control of the mind which becomes "concentrated in emptiness, while the whole personality is calmed by the rhythmic breathing which in itself is one of the oldest forms of therapy known."[24] Another distinctive element of Zen is the *koan* which is a difficult problem posed by the Zen master, often in the form of an enigma with a paradoxical twist, that must be solved by the pupil if he is to have *satori*. Finally, one must be detached from one's own ego, in order to bring about a great interior silence that brings about "mind expansion and an extraordinary psychic unity in which true wisdom or *satori* is obtained."[25] The theoretical basis for Zen lies at the very roots of Buddhism in the Four Noble Truths where it is stated that desire is the cause of all illusion and suffering. For this reason it is believed that all desire must be completely eliminated if one is to find true wisdom.

Although the underlying theory of St. John of the Cross is quite different, the *nadas* of his ascetical doctrine are remarkably similar in practice—detachment from all things even from the concepts and images leading to the interior silence of contemplation. St. John is not propounding a theory of his own but speaks as a representative of a long Christian tradition of the apophatic theology of darkness stemming from Dionysius. To this tradition belong the Rhineland mystics and the anonymous author of the *Cloud of Unknowing*. However, the roots can be traced back to St. Augustine of Hippo, St. Gregory of Nyssa, and the Scriptures where we find the greatest mystic of all, Jesus Himself. In modern times, a basically similar doctrine can be found in the pages of Thomas Merton, Jacques Maritain, and T. S. Eliot.[26] Remarking on the doctrine of the void, Maritain remarks that it "would be absurd, were God not supernaturally present in the soul..., were God not there knocking at the gate, to invade the soul wholly, to replace all it has lost by a better life which is the life of God Himself, the torrent of his peace."[27] St. John's uniqueness in the apophatic tradition lies in his treatment of the theological virtues as a means of making a void within one's self. This void enables "the living flame of love" that rises in the depth of the heart to grow into "a raging fire that envelops the whole personality and governs every action of one's life."[28]

Comparing these two experiences, both entail a complete detachment and a unification of the personality, though the unifying principle in each case is different. Where in St. John of the Cross it is a unifying love that rises in the heart as a result of meditation on Holy Scripture and the life of Christ, based on a love that springs from the fullness of Christian wisdom, in Zen, it is a complete annihilation of the person, independent of any love experience. For St. John of the Cross, until this love exists in some rudimentary form, reasoning and thinking should not be abandoned in discursive prayer until one can legitimately pass into the prayer of silence.[29] However, in Zen, there is nothing of this nor is there mention of anything like the "living flame of love."

Moreover, there is a great similarity between these two experiences as forms of concentration, but the difference lies in that which induces the state of concentration. In Zen, the concentration is artificially provoked by the breathing, the sitting, the beating, and an irrational *koan*, as well as a tremendous effort to rid oneself of all suppositions, whether metaphysical or dogmatic. In Christian mysticism, however, the suppositions are the key to the whole process. They are faith in and love for Christ which have been nurtured normally for years until something radical happens quite unexpectedly. In the latter, one cannot think because of the strength of the "living flame of love" that has arisen in the heart. Here, the concentration has been induced by a burning love rising out of faith; and the ligature has been caused precisely by this love and faith.[30]

Just as *satori* is the center of Zen, so infused contemplation is traditionally the center of Christian religious life. Possibly the frequent talk about enlightenment in Zen could have blinded many to infused contemplation. This is the Christian enlightenment which is centuries old and which built Western Christianity.[31]

Christians who possess an authentic Christian faith, cannot sit at the feet of a Zen master and obtain enlightenment just as it has been handed down from the time of Bodhidharma. Enlightenment is not an isolated moment, but part of the complete texture of a person's life. It is impossible for Christian enlightenment to be found independently of Holy Scripture, the Mass, and the Sacraments; for these are the components of Christian enlightenment.[32] Besides, the Western psyche cannot take on the Eastern enlightenment. According to Jung, the psychologist, the "mental education necessary for Zen was lacking in the West and that a direct transplantation to Western conditions was neither commendable nor possible."[33]

The Jesus Movement

Possibly one of the most amazing of all the movements of our time involves virtually thousands of young people who call themselves, "the Jesus freaks" or "the Jesus people." Their prominence is witnessed through evangelization on the streets, on campuses, and sometimes in churches.[34]

This youth movement apparently has the zeal and some of the methods of Hare Krishna but with Jesus, not Krishna, in the center of it. Though their form of celebration is innovative, it contains much traditional substance.

Like the Eastern religions, it speaks out against drugs and yearns for a more satisfying personal religion other than its adherents see in the religion of their parents.[35]

Seemingly "the Jesus people" are motivated by an unrecognized need for a strong father-figure, as well as an external authority to reduce personal tensions. Their motivations also include a search for an encounter with the transcendent and the widespread longing for community. Seeking alternative and substitute experiences, however, some are involved with drugs. Many in the movement reflect a trend to separatism for youth; though this may simply be another fad. Yet for some it may well be a genuine religious experience prompted and guided by the Holy Spirit.[36] Still their convictions seem paramount: that Jesus saves, and has brought these young people to a new meaning and purpose in life; that Jesus calls them to witness to their faith in every available circumstance and manner; and that the Bible is their only source of truth and authority.[37]

Formerly these thousands of young people professed indifference or scorn toward religion. There is clear evidence of the power of Jesus to capture the imagination of persons in any generation, for "the light shines in the darkness, and the darkness has not overcome it." Doubtless in the lives of many, a genuine transformation has been wrought. According to those who have visited the Christian communes, reports are that their ethical fruits seem wholesome, and there is a serious concern for mutual helpfulness. Usually there is a Pentecostal fervor of joy in the Lord and new life in Christ. However, at times, their experiences seem greatly heightened by the use of various kinds of drugs and hallucinogens, the most popular being marijuana. Despite this let-down in a reflection of their ideals, converts off drugs testify that their decision for Jesus, and the experiences of a supernatural power beyond human control is what gives them release and freedom never before known.

The experience of being born again in Jesus seemed to be the only valid explanation any of them could give.[38]

A great vehicle of the Jesus Movement is music. Jesus rock and gospel melodies generate rich, powerful feelings in this emotion-oriented age and hold the movement together. "It is largely music that has made the movement a part of pop culture," writes Ellwood, "and it is the Jesus movement as pop culture that distinguishes it from what is going on in the churches."[39]

Through a decade of suspicion, the Jesus Movement has survived. It is far stronger than the faddism attributed to it by its first observers, or by the mass circulation journals. It has also survived because it is far more complex a movement than an old time revivalism. Jesus has been made intelligible in terms of their own needs, as a great liberator from oppression and as a friend and lover who expects nothing in return. He is the only one who could save them from destroying themselves.[40]

With this sense of liberation, "the Jesus people" cannot keep their new-found faith among themselves to be brought out only on Sunday morning or at a mid-week "youth rally." Even though this movement has many good points, these young people are searching for new personal and social expressions of their faith to be accomplished in their own way, freed from any ties with traditional religious observance.

The Catholic Pentecostals

Within the Catholic Church, as in other established churches, it seems that the charismatic renewal responds to the thirst of our contemporary society by bringing people to genuine religious experience. Moreover, this experience is not procured or sought by means of psychosomatic, superstitious methods, nor by devices of any sort, but simply by faith. Indeed, there are, and no doubt will always be, Pentecostals who seek religious experience for its own sake, but this is an error which those who have a true sense of the workings of the Spirit readily recognize. Presupposing proper Christian goals of fulfilling God's will, it remains true that personal experience of God has a genuine role to play in Christian life. Father O'Conner claims that the "experience, which so many seek in the wrong places today, is being realized in the charismatic renewal by those who surrender themselves wholeheartedly to the guidance of faith."[41]

Dr. J. Massingberd Ford, an authority on the Catholic Pentecostal Movement in the United States, says that one of the emerging features in the Pentecostal Movement which should be given a great deal of prayerful and intelligent consideration is the "baptism of the Holy Spirit." Ford explains that the "baptism of the Spirit" is not a state of infused contemplation, but rather only a touch of infused contemplation, "naturally accompanied by an experimental sense of the presence of God and of His intimate love, with or without the gift of tongues." Although the duration of this experience varies considerably in individuals, it is probably of extremely short duration in most people. What is commonly believed to be a continuation of release of the Spirit may well be more aptly called "sensible devotion," which Ford describes as a "rich and fervent devotion accompanied by healthy religious emotion." This is not to deny the work of the Holy Spirit, but at the same time this experience is not due to the direct intervention of God; therefore it cannot be described as "infused contemplation." This devotion may last for varying periods and is usually followed by times of dryness in prayer, after which an experience of silent waiting in the presence of God ensues.[42] However, there is no set program for religious experience.

Throughout her writings, St. Teresa of Avila says that many attain high degrees of spiritual maturity with no such experience. She also says that at the highest levels of spiritual attainment the soul is at rest in its depths. The Zen

Masters claim that the "perfect" man is the one who, to all external appearances, is the ordinary man—"a reflection of the stability of the Divine Life itself, unmoved by anything except moment-by-moment attentiveness to his True Nature, the Spirit directing from within." It would seem to follow that experiences such as the "Spirit-baptism" which may occur at any time, as a general rule, are more likely to occur in the early stages of spiritual growth. Psychology confirms that "the more unconscious the forces have been integrated into the totality of the personality, the less likely and more refined are so-called 'outbursts of affect.'"[43] Nonetheless, if "Spirit-baptism" is a touch of infused contemplation, then it is a privilege and a gift solely due to the will of God and not to any human effort. Even though one may dispose oneself to such an experience in faith, hope, and love, one can neither demand it nor decide what form it should take.

At a meeting of the Association of Contemplative Nuns, a Pentecostal theologian, himself a recipient of "the baptism of the Holy Spirit," was questioned about the relevance of the "Spirit-baptism" to religious. He replied that it was quite relevant to most religious because of the culture in which they have been brought up. Many religious had attained to a high degree of the spiritual life with little if any "Spirit-awareness." These religious have been "the victims of the Western cultural vacuum against which Pentecostalism is a reaction," and partly because of this, "religious life has not always been the ongoing growth process it was intended to be from its historical beginnings."[44]

However, some Catholic Pentecostals are making a mistake by expecting people in different stages of prayer to return to their early experiences. Because it is quite impossible to return to "sensible devotion" in some states of prayer, many are made to feel very anxious and sometimes inferior because they do not experience the "dramatic" manifestations of the Holy Spirit. "Some spiritual experiences are too subtle or refined to be felt by the emotions."[45]

Others may impede spiritual growth and prevent individual development by attempting to keep people in a state of "sensible devotion" too long, or by trying to "work this up" by community prayer which lays "great stress on hymn singing, guitar playing, clapping of hands, use of the gift of tongues and exhortations charged with rather too much emotion." Such procedures may limit the time for listening to God as He speaks silently in the depths of one's being.[46] When one is called to the prayer of quiet, not only the emotional exuberance of joy in the Spirit must be suspended, but even discursive meditation must cease.[47] The Neo-Pentecostal Movement certainly brings with it "sensible devotion," which in itself is good, but which will be accompanied by temptations which St. John of the Cross describes in the opening chapters of the *Dark Night*.

That revivalism in various forms does occur when social and religious structures break down and when faith becomes secularized, can be verified by history. No matter how good and grace-bearing this revivalism may be, one must be cognizant of the fact that the Pentecostal experience is accompanied by enthusiasm and even sometimes by fanaticism, and that the large numbers involved make the movement very difficult to control. Pentecostalism needs the help of Christian humanists, of the arts and sciences, of structured liturgical practices, and of a fuller understanding of the Scriptures in terms of wholly integrated and intelligent standards.[48]

The Relevance of Teresian Spiritual Theology

Since there is no need to marshal further evidence for the contemporary interest in mysticism, one needs to examine this phenomenon in light of its relationship to Teresian Spiritual Theology.

The Chicago Sun-Times printed an article about the frustrations of angry and disenchanted young people "who gave up family and friends—and months or years of their lives—to join religious cults and follow new messiahs." These young people discovered that the Hare Krishna Movement and other cults as well were not only lacking in the challenges and expectations of true mystical experience, but were decisively based on fraudulent fund-raising.[49] Impoverished by a faith in false idols, superstitious signs, and pseudo-mystical experiences, they are once again seeking the true God from whom they temporarily turned away. Without doubt the writings of Teresa would help them tremendously in their search for intimacy with the Divine.

Some of the experiences described by the addicts are so similar to those described by St. Teresa in the upper Dwelling Places of the *Interior Castle* that both kinds of experiences are sometimes referred to as mystical. However, where the addict finds pleasure in bodily sensations, the mystic finds fulfillment in being united with God. Where the addict is uplifted by a self-initiated high-mental condition, the mystic remains passive and is elevated by the movement of God Himself. Where the addict turns inward on himself, the mystic becomes completely open to the will of God. The simplicity and ineffability of the mystic's experience is what makes it incomparable to any humanly induced condition.[50] Furthermore, the true mystical descent into the core of the mystic "is always accompanied by progress in moral virtue and in psychic maturity, and it effects a reform or a conversion...but in the use of drugs no such moral change is evident," nor is there any effect showing "detachment and the serenity resulting from silent meditation."[51] In chapter three of the Fifth Dwelling Places, St. Teresa insists that the Christian must concentrate the great part of his attention throughout the entire spiritual life on practical virtue, and above all on love—the essence of the Christian religion.[52]

In dealing with the Eastern religions, a question arises whether it is possible for man to have a true experience of God outside the Christian faith. In pre-Christian centuries and in contemporary India, there seem to be wise men who have had a direct experience of God. *In Sagesse Hindoue, mystique chrisfienne,* Le Saux claims that man can have a true experience of God outside the Christian faith for the Holy Spirit breathes where He wills. He mentions Noah, Abraham, Job, and Daniel as holy men of the epoch of Cosmic Religion and Sri Ramana Maharishi (1879-1950) as a contemporary of immense religious import. Le Saux defines cosmic religion as "essentially the contemplation and adoration of God in manifestations of the cosmic order: in nature, in man, in the heart of man, in the inmost recesses of his heart, and finally at the very source of his being." He further maintains that this is still "the normal and providential meeting place between God and man where the Messiah is not yet known." [53]

On the other hand, the Christian aim is union with God by an incorporation with the Mystical Body of Christ through baptism, and by a union of the will with the divine will through one's duties in life. Moreover, an ever deepening union through the dynamism of sanctifying grace and the gifts of the Holy Spirit can lead to a most profound union with the indwelling Trinity. If the Eastern pioneer of prayer has a true experience of God, in comparison to the infinitely richer experience of the Christian mystic to whom God reveals Himself as Trinity, the former is quite limited to say the least.

A renewed interest in the Humanity of Christ which has been sparked by biblical studies in particular, has found its way into the Jesus Movement as well. Though its doctrines are vaguely defined, its adherents would do well to read the timeless works of St. Teresa, who so vividly speaks of the Humanity of Jesus, with emphasis on His love as a Person. What St. Teresa wrote about the Humanity of

Christ four centuries ago, writes Father Bourne, "is so beautiful and so true that not one word needs to be changed." The love of the Person of Jesus permeates her whole doctrine.[54] Since the articulations of "the Jesus people" are Christ-centered rather than creed-oriented, St. Teresa's approach to the Humanity of Christ in her writings would serve as a clarification of their supernatural and eschatological views.

A knowledge of Teresian spiritual theology can save much grief and provide much benefit for the Pentecostal. Her theology recognizes that God may occasionally instruct some souls by means of extraordinary gifts, but stresses that such gifts of themselves do not bring a person into union with God. A contemporary statement confirming the Teresian position is that of *Lumen gentium:*

> Extraordinary gifts are not to be sought after, nor are the fruits of apostolic labor to be presumptuously expected from their use.[55]

When the Lord deepens the faith life of His people by withholding some of His gifts in order to bring them into the deeper ways of contemplative prayer, the Teresian guidelines are invaluable.

In the *Dictionary of the Bible* Father McKenzie compares the influence of the Carmelite Doctors to that of the prophets by saying:

> The only satisfactory parallel to the prophetic experience is the phenomena of mysticism as described by writers like Teresa of Avila, John of the Cross, and others. They affirm that the immediate experience of God is ineffable; like the prophets, they describe it as a transforming experience which moves one to speech and action beyond one's expected capacities. It grants them a profound insight not only into divine reality but into the human scene. Thus the prophetic experience is such a mystical immediate experience of the reality and presence of God.[56]

Although public revelation has come to a close with the death of the last Apostles, St. Teresa and St. John of the Cross are considered prophets because they bear in the Church a personal testimony to the reality of God and Christ in the might of His Spirit. If we read these authentic records of communion with God our spiritual sensibility will certainly quicken. "To live for a time with the interpretations of life created by the world's greatest masters of it in literature, music or painting," writes the scholar E. Allison Peers, "is never again to find complete satisfaction in inferior company."[57] So, too, once our taste for the spiritual is formed on the works of the Mystical Doctors, our standards of life will be raised to a higher level and nothing of lesser worth will ever satisfy us again.

Teresa, who also lived during a time of renewal in the Church, was led by God to see that a life of prayer is the place where the renewal of the Church should begin. Consequently, Teresa teaches us to see the whole spiritual life and the life of the Church in the perspective of prayer and contemplation. The freedom that Teresian prayer allows us in our personal communication with God is certainly in keeping with the present-day atmosphere. Concerning all of human life, Teresa believed that all life is worthwhile only when one is in love. Hence, she found the true meaning of a happy and useful life, had a sense of solidarity with others, while being totally anchored in God. Likewise Marcel points out, that only by living in the fullness of love can one feel that life has meaning.[58] Undoubtedly, this is exactly what millions are seeking today.

A renewal of interest in the life and the ascesis of St. Teresa, a true "daughter of the Church," will be a renewal of interest in the life of Christ and of the Church since her life and ascesis are but a reflection and an echo of the Gospels. This would certainly lead to the new Pentecost that was so greatly desired by Pope John XXIII. That Teresa has much to tell us as she dialogues with the contemporary world is presented most pointedly by Hoornaert:

> St. Teresa has, by her writings, opened new horizons to the human race, and let in a breath of fresh air on men ever too much inclined to narrow, material and immediate solutions. Her description of states of soul, her explorations of the inner world which every man bears about within him, have caused a great wind of idealism to blow over the human race and ventilate the world. Hence we believe that St. Teresa's genius...has not merely enriched but greatly enlarged the patrimony of the human race by supplying it with treasures of Divine Truth wrapped in the golden mantle of Beauty.[59]

FOOTNOTES

1. Edward D. O'Connor, C.S.C., *Pentecost in the Modern World*, (Notre Dame, Indiana: Ave Maria Press, 1972), 26-27.

2. Keith J. Egan, O. Carm., "Mysticism, Mystical Theology, and American Culture" (unpublished manuscript of Fr. Egan, Assistant Professor of Historical Theology and Spirituality, Theology Department, Marquette University, Milwaukee, Summer, 1975), 13.

3. Georgia Harkness, *Mysticism: Its Meaning and Message* (Nashville, Tenn.: Abington Press, 1973), 160.

4. *Ibid.*, 161.

5. Philip Schmidt, S.J., *Superstition and Magic*, trans. by Marie Herrerman and Rev. A. J. Peeler (Westminster, Md.: The Newman Press, 1963), 18.

6. *Ibid.*, 19.

7. *Ibid.*, 19-20.

8. *Ibid.*, 14.

9. J. D. Fearon, "Superstition," *New Catholic Encyclopedia*, 1967, XIII, 818.

10. Hal Bridges, *American Mysticism: From William James to Zen* (New York: Harper, 1970), 151, Appendix A. Statement by Swami Prabhavananda.

11. *Ibid.*, 152.

12. William James, *The Varieties of Religious Experience*, with a Foreword by Jacques Barzun (New York: New American Library of World Literature, 1958), 298.

13. Harkness, *Mysticism*, 162-164.

14. William Johnston, *The Mysticism of the Cloud of Unknowing: A Modern Interpretation*, with a Foreword by Thomas Merton (New York: Desclee Company, 1967), xiii.

15. Kieran Kavanaugh, O.C.D., "LSD and Religious Experience—II; A Theologian's Viewpoint," *Spiritual Life*, xiii (Spring, 1967), 63.

16. J.F. Staal and A.C. Bhaktivedanta Swami, *The Krsna Consciousness Movement Is the Genuine Vedic Way* (Boston: ISKCON Press, 1970), 2.

17. Harkness, *Mysticism*, 168.

18. Sister Marie Hamelin, R.J.M., "Yoga—Yes or No?" *Review for Religious*, xxx (July, 1974), 818.

19. H. E. Meyers, "Yoga," *New Catholic Encyclopedia*, 1967, XIV, 1071.

20. *Ibid.*

21. *Ibid.*, 1072.

22. Thomas L. Campbell, C.S.C., "Prayer in the Eastern Religions," *Sisters Today*, xl (December, 1973), 210.

23. Rammurti Mishra, *Fundamentals of Yoga* (New York: Lancer, 1969), 61.

24. William Johnston, *The Still Point: Reflections on Zen and Christian Mysticism* (New York: Harper & Row Publishers, 1971), 5.

25. William Johnston, S.J., "Zen and Christian Contemplation," *Review for Religious*, xxix (September, 1970), 699-700.

26. Johnston, *Still Point*, 28.

27. Jacques Maritain, *The Degrees of Knowledge*, translated from the fourth French edition under the supervision of Gerald B. Phelan, 331. Copyright © 1959 Jacques Maritain. Reprinted with the permission of Charles Scribner's Sons.

28. Johnston, "Zen and Christian Contemplation," 701.

29. *Ibid.*, 81.

30. Johnston, *Still Point*, 84.

31. Johnston, "Zen and Christian Contemplation," 703.

32. *Ibid.*, 704.

33. C. G. Jung, *Psychology and Religion: West and East*, trans. by R. F. C. Hull, Bollinger Series XX (New York: Pantheon Books, Inc., 1958), 537.

34. Harkness, *Mysticism*, 174-175.

35. *Ibid.*

36. Father Lawrence Murphy, "The Jesus Movement: A Critique," *Catholic Mind*, lxxi (March, 1973), 4.

37. Harkness, *Mysticism*, 176.

38. Erling T. Jorstad, "From Drugs to Jesus," *Catholic Mind*, lxx (December, 1972), 18.

39. Robert S. Ellwood Jr., *One Way: The Jesus Movement and Its Meaning* © 1973, 63-64. Reprinted by permission of Prentice-Hall, Inc., Englewood Cliffs, New Jersey.

40. Jorstad, *"From Drugs to Jesus,"* 20-21.

41. O'Connor, *Pentecost in the Modern World*, 27-28.

42. Dr. J. Massingberd Ford, "Fly United—But Not in Too Close Formation: Reflections on the Catholic Pentecostal Movement," *Spiritual Life*, xvii (Spring, 1970), 12-13; cf. Above, 80.

43. Anthony Haglof, O.C.D., "On Spirit-Baptism and Religious Commitment," manuscript, Peterborough, N.H., June, 1974, 3-4.

44. *Ibid.*, 2.

45. Ford, "Fly United," 14.

46. *Ibid.*

47. *Ibid.,* 33ff.

48. Ford, "Fly United," 19-20.

49. Peter Arnett, "Disenchanted Young People Throw Off the Cult Life," *Chicago Sun-Times,* Thursday, December 25, 1975, 54.

50. Cf. R. C. Zaechner, *Zen, Drugs and Mysticism* (New York: Pantheon House, 1972), 113ff.

51. Johnston, *Still Point,* 147.

52. *Interior Castle,* V, 3; Kavanaugh-Rodriguez, II, 348-349.

53. Hamelin, "Yoga—Yes or No?" 825.

54. Peter Bourne, O.C.D., "St. Teresa and the Person of Jesus," manuscript, Peterborough, N.H., 1.

55. "Lumen gentium," *Dogmatic Constitution on the Church,* 12, the sixteen documents of Vatican II, N.C. translation (Boston: St. Paul Editions, 1967), 122.

56. John L. McKenzie, *Dictionary of the Bible,* 697. Copyright © 1965 by The Bruce Publishing Co. Reprinted with permission of Macmillan Publishing Co.

57. Peers, *Spirit of Flame,* 206-207.

58. Father Michael Griffin, O.C.D., "Saint Teresa, Doctor of the Church," *Spiritual Life,* xvi (Winter, 1970), 239.

59. R. Hoornaert, *Saint Teresa in Her Writings,* trans. by Rev. J. Leonard, C.M. (New York: Benziger Bros., 1931), 377-378.

Select Bibliography

St. Teresa of Avila

BOOKS

Albarran, A. De Castro. *The Dust of Her Sandals*. Translated by Sister Mary Bernarda, B.V.M., Mundelein College, Chicago, Illinois. Chicago: Benziger Brothers, 1936.

Auclair, Marcelle. *Teresa of Avila*. Translated by Kathleen Pond with a preface by Andre Maurois. Garden City, New York: Doubleday & Co., Inc., 1961.

Beevers, John Leonard. *St. Teresa of Avila*. Garden City, New York: Hanover House, 1961.

Brice, Rev. *Teresa, John, and Therese*. New York: Frederick Pustet Co., 1946.

Bruno of Jesus Mary, O.C.D. *Three Mystics: El Greco, St. John of the Cross and St. Teresa*. Edited by Father Bruno of Jesus Mary, O.C.D. New York: Sheed and Ward, 1949.

Butler. "St. Teresa of Avila: Virgin, Foundress of the Discalced Carmelites," *Butler's Lives of the Saints*. Vol. IV. Complete edition, edited, revised and supplemented by Herbert Thurston, S.J. and Donald Attwater. New York: P.J. Kennedy and Sons, 1956, 111-121.

Chesterton, Mrs. Cecil. *St. Teresa*. Garden City, New York: Doubleday, Doran and Company, Inc., 1928.

Cognet, Louis. "St. Teresa of Avila," *Post-Reformation Spirituality*. Translated from the French by P. Hepburne Scott. New York: Hawthorne Books, Publishers, 1959, 36-44.

Crisogono, Father, O.C.D. *Saint Teresa of Jesus: Her Life and Her Ascetico-Mystical Doctrine*. Adapted by Father Stanislaus of Jesus, O.C.D. India: Alwaye, 1939.

Dicken, E. W. Trueman. *The Crucible of Love: A Study of the Mysticism of St. Teresa of Jesus and St. John of the Cross*. New York: Sheed and Ward, 1963.

An Anglican view of the two great Spanish mystics.

Farges, Albert. *Mystical Phenomena*. London: Burns, Oates and Wash-
bourne, 1926.
    A treatise on Mystical Theology according to the principles of
St. Teresa.
_____. *The Ordinary Ways of the Spiritual Life*. New York:
Benziger Bros., 1927.
    A treatise on ascetical theology according to the principles of
St. Teresa declared by the Carmelite Congress of Madrid (March,
1923) for the use of seminaries, the clergy and lay people.
Francois of Saint Mary, Father, O.C.D. *The Simple Steps to God*. Wilkes-
Barre, Penn.: Dimension Books, 1943.
Fulop-Miller, Rene. *The Saints That Moved the World: Anthony,
Augustine, Francis, Ignatius, Theresa*. Translated by Alexander
Gode and Erika Fulop-Miller. New York: Thomas Y. Cromwell
Co., 1947.
Gabriel of St. Mary Magdalen, O.C.D. *Saint Teresa of Jesus*. Translated
from the Italian by a Benedictine of Stanbrook Abbey. Westmin-
ster, Md.: Newman Press, 1949.
_____. *Visions and Revelations in the Spiritual Life*. Translated
by a Benedictine of Stanbrook Abbey. Westminster, Md.: New-
man Press, 1950.
_____. *The Way of Prayer: A Commentary on St. Teresa's "Way
of Perfection."* Translated by the Carmel of Baltimore. Milwaukee:
Spiritual Life Press, 1965.
Graef, Hilda. *The Light and the Rainbow*. Westminster, Md.: Newman
Press, 1959, 310-352.
Hamilton, Elizabeth. *The Great Teresa*. London: Chatto and Windus,
1960.
_____. *Saint Teresa: A Journey in Spain*. New York: Charles
Scribner's Sons, 1959.
Hatzfeld, Helmut A. *Santa Teresa de Avila*. New York: Twayne
Publishers, Inc., 1969.
Hoornaert, R. *Saint Teresa in Her Writings*. Translated by Reverend J.
Leonard, C.M. New York: Benziger Bros., 1931.
Hough, Mary E. *Saint Teresa in America*. New York: Hispanic Institute,
1938.
Hughes, Catherine, ed. *Prison of Love: Selections from St. Teresa of Avila*.
Mysticism and Modern Man Series, Vol. I. New York: Sheed and
Ward, 1972.
Kelly, Joseph P. *Meet Saint Teresa: An Introduction to "La Madre" of
Avila*. New York: Frederick Pustet Co., 1958.
Kranz, Gisbert. "Teresa of Avila," *The Modern Christian Literature*.
Translated from the French by J. R. Foster, New York: Haw-
thorne Books, Publishers, 1961, 27-32.
Lavelle, Louis. *The Meaning of Holiness: As Exemplified in Four Saints:
St. Francis of Assisi, St. Teresa of Avila, St. John of the Cross, and
St. Francis de Sales*. New York: Pantheon Books, 1954.

Lewis, D. *Saint Teresa*. London: Catholic Truth Society, 1958.

Lewis, Sister Mary Regina, O.C.D. *Saint Teresa of Jesus: Undaunted Daughter of Desires*. Long Beach, California: Carmel of Saint Joseph, n.d.

Lovat, Alice Lady. *The Life of Saint Teresa*. Taken from the French—with a Preface by Msgr. Robert Hugh Benson. St. Louis, Mo.: B. Herder, 1912.

McKenzie, John L. *Dictionary of the Bible*. New York: Macmillan Publishing Co., 1965, 697.

Marie-Eugene, P., O.C.D. *I Want to See God: A Practical Synthesis of Carmelite Spirituality*. Vol. I. Translated by Sister M. Verda Clare, C.S.C. Chicago: Fides Publishers Association, 1955.

_____. *I Am a Daughter of the Church: A Practical Synthesis of Carmelite Spirituality*. Vol. II. Translated by Sister M. Verda Clare, C.S.C. Chicago: Fides Publishers Association, 1955.

Mary of the Blessed Sacrament, O.C.D. *A Retreat Under the Guidance of St. Teresa*. Prefaced by a letter of commendation by Cardinal Mercier. London: Burns & Oates, 1929.

Moriones, Ildefonso, O.C.D. *The Teresian Charism: A Study of the Origins*. Translated by Christopher O'Mahony, O.C.D. Rome: Teresianum, 1972.

Nevin, Winifred. *Heirs of St. Teresa of Avila*. Milwaukee: Bruce Publishing Company, 1959.

_____. *Teresa of Avila, the Woman*. New York: Sheed and Ward, 1951.

O'Brien, Kate. *Teresa of Avila*. New York: Sheed and Ward, 1951.

Papasogli, Giorgio. *St. Teresa of Avila*. Translated from the Italian by G. Anzilotti. New York: Society of St. Paul, 1959.

Peers, E. Allison. *Behind the Wall: An Introduction to Some Classics of the Interior Life*. Toronto: Macmillan Co., 1947.

_____. Handbook to the Life and Times of St. Teresa and St. John of the Cross. Westminster, Md.: Newman Press, 1954.

_____. *Mother of Carmel: A Portrait of St. Teresa of Jesus*. New York: Morehouse-Gorham, 1946.

_____. *St. Teresa of Jesus and Other Essays and Addresses*. London: Faber and Faber, 1953.

_____. *Spain, the Church and the Orders*. London: Burns Oates & Washbourne Ltd., 1945.

_____. Spanish Mysticism. London: Methuen & Co. Ltd., 1924.

_____. *Studies of the Spanish Mystics*. 2 vols. London: S.P.C.K., 1930-1960.

Peers, E. Allison, ed. *Spain: A Companion to Spanish Studies*, 2nd ed., with three maps. London: Methuen & Co. Ltd., 1930.

Petersson, Robert T. *The Art of Ecstacy: Teresa, Bernini, and Crashaw*. Atheneum, New York: The Murray Printing Co., 1970.

Pourrat, Pierre, S. S. *Christian Spirituality*. Vol. III: *From the Renaissance to Jansenism*. Translated by W. H. Mitchell and others. Westminster, Md.: Newman Press, 1922-1955.

Ramge, Sebastian V. *An Introduction to the Writings of St. Teresa.* Chicago: H. Regnery, 1963.

Sullivan, John J., S.J. *God and the Interior Life*. Boston: St. Paul Editions, 1961, 101-109.

Teresa of Jesus, Saint. *The Collected Works of St. Teresa of Avila.* 2 vols. Translated and edited by Kieran Kavanaugh and Otilio Rodriguez. Washington, D.C.: ICS Publications, 1976 and 1980.

—————————. *The Complete Works of Saint Teresa of Jesus.* 3 vols. Translated and edited by E. Allison Peers from the critical edition of P. Silverio de Santa Teresa, C.D. New York: Sheed and Ward, 1946.

—————————. *The Letters of Saint Teresa of Jesus.* 2 vols. Translated and edited by E. Allison Peers from the critical edition of P. Silverio de Santa Teresa, C.D. Westminster, Md.: Newman Press, 1950.

—————————. *The Life of St. Teresa of Jesus*. Translated from the Spanish by David Lewis, re-edited with additional notes and introduction by the Very Rev. Benedict Zimmerman, O.C.D. Westminster, Md.: Newman Press, 1944.

Teresita Marie, Sister, O.C.D. *The Legacy of Saint Teresa of Avila: A Minor Concordance of Her Works and Writings,* Santa Fe, New Mexico: Carmelite Monastery, n.d.

Thomas, Father, O.D.C. ed. *St. Teresa of Avila: Studies in Her Life, Doctrine and Times.* Dublin: Clonmore and Reynolds, Ltd., 1963.

Walsh, William Thomas. *Saint Teresa of Avila: A Biography*. Milwaukee: Bruce Publishing Company, 1943.

ARTICLES

Bourne, Peter, O.C.D. "St. Teresa and the Person of Jesus," manuscript, Peterborough, New Hampshire, June, 1974.

Britto, John, C.M.I. "Saint Teresa and Oriental Spirituality," *Eucharist and Priest,* LXVIII (1962), 291-302.

Christopher, Father, O.C.D. "Fourth Centenary of the Teresian Reform of Carmel," *Spiritual Life,* VIII, 2 (Summer, 1962), 74-77.

"The Church Has Doctors Who Are Women," *Mary the Messenger,* English edition, translated by Mary of Jesus, no. 3, n.d.

Del Monte Sol, Teresa. "Teresa and Our Times," *Spiritual Life,* XVI, 4 (Winter, 1970), 247-252.

Dicken, E. W. T. "The Imagery of the Interior Castle and Its Implications," *Ephemerides Carmeliticae,* V, 21 (1970), 198-218.

—————————. "St. Teresa of Jesus and the New Spirituality," *Mount Carmel,* (Spring, 1972), 193-203.

"Doctor of the Church: A Reflection on St. Teresa," *L'Osservatore Romano,* English edition, n. 40 (131) October 1, 1970, p. 1.

Dohen, Dorothy. "St. Teresa and Common Sense," *Spiritual Life,* V, 3 (September, 1959), 218-225.

Dougherty, John, S.S. "St. Teresa of Avila, a Most Excellent Spiritual Teacher," *The Wanderer,* October 12, 1972, p. 3.

Gabriel of St. Mary Magdalen, Father, O.C.D. "Characteristics of Teresian Spirituality," *Spiritual Life,* I, 1 (March, 1955), 36-55.

Griffin, Michael, O.C.D. "Saint Teresa, Doctor of the Church," *Spiritual Life,* XVI, 4 (Winter, 1970), 226-246.

Larkin, Ernest E., O. Carm. "Saint Teresa of Avila and Women's Liberation," *Sisters Today,* XLV, 9 (May, 1974), 562-568.

Latimer, Christopher, O.C.D. "The Prayer of St. Teresa Today," *Spiritual Life,* XIV, 2 (Summer, 1968), 91-97.

Long, T. K., C.SS.R. "Saint Teresa of Avila: St. Alphonsus' Second Mother," *Eucharist and Priest,* LXVIII (1962), 312-317.

Luke, Sister Mary, C.S.J. "Teresa of Avila: In the Spirit of St. Alphonsus," *Liguorian,* LXI, 4 (April, 1973), 55-58.

M.M.B. "St. Teresa of Avila," *Strain Forward,* VI, 9 (October, 1973), 12-18.

"A Marian Way of Life," brochure describing the way of life of the Third Order of the Discalced Carmelites, disseminated by the Discalced Carmelites of Milwaukee.

O'Brien, Kate. "Teresa of Avila," *The Critic,* XXXVI, 2 (Winter, 1975), 26-51.

O'Donoghue, N. D., O.D.C. "Your Servant Teresa," *Furrow,* (1973), 409-419.

Otilio, Father, O.D.C. "St. Teresa of Avila, Mother and Lawgiver," *Spiritual Life,* VIII, 2 (Summer, 1962), 78-91.

Paul VI, Pope. "Address during the Ceremony of Proclamation of St. Teresa of Avila as Doctor of the Church," *L'Osservatore Romano,* English edition, n. 41 (132), October 8, 1970, pp. 6-7.

_____. "Teresa of Avila: The Message of Prayer," *The Pope Speaks,* XV, 3 (Autumn, 1970), 218-222.

_____. "The Teresian Art of Praying," *Spiritual Life,* XIX, 2 (Summer, 1973), 82-87.

Rodriguez, Otilio, O.C.D. "Saint Teresa of Jesus: First Woman Doctor of the Church," *Spiritual Life,* XVI, 4 (Winter, 1970), 213-225.

Schaefer, Thomas E. "Common Sense and Saint Teresa," *Cross and Crown.* XVIII, 1 (March, 1966), 68-74.

Smith, Thomas B. "A Lay Carmelite Witness to Teresian Essentials," *Spiritual Life,* XVIII, 2 (Summer, 1972), 118-127.

Stillmock, Rev. Martin A., C.SS.R. "St. Alphonsus and St. Teresa of Avila," *Spiritual Life,* X, 4 (Winter, 1963), 260-266.

Welch, Romaine, O.C.D. "The Heart of the Teresian Vocation," *Spiritual Life,* XVI, 4 (Winter, 1970), 261-263.

St. John of the Cross

BOOKS

Brice, Father, C.P. *Journey in the Night: A Practical Introduction to St. John of the Cross, and, in Particular a Companion to the First Book of the "Ascent of Mt. Carmel."* New York: Frederick Pustet Co., 1945.

——————. *Spirit in Darkness: A Companion to Book Two of the "Ascent of Mt. Carmel."* New York: Frederick Pustet Co., Inc., 1946.

Bruno, Fr., O.D.C. *St. John of the Cross.* Edited by Fr. Benedict Zimmerman, O.D.C., with an introduction by Jacques Maritain. New York: Benziger Brothers, 1932.

Cognet, Louis. "St. John of the Cross," *Post-Reformation Spirituality.* Translated from the French by P. Hepbourne Scott. New York: Hawthorne Books, Publishers, 1959, 44-51.

Crisogono de Jesus, O.C.D. *The Life of St. John of the Cross.* Translated by Kathleen Pond. New York: Harper & Brothers, 1958.

Cristiani, Leon. *St. John of the Cross, Prince of Mystical Theology.* Translated from the French. Garden City, New York: Doubleday & Company, Inc., 1962.

Diefenbach, Gabriel. *Common Mystic Prayer.* Paterson, N.J.: St. Anthony Guild Press, 1947, 108-120.

Frost, Bede, O.S.B. *St. John of the Cross, Doctor of Divine Love: An Introduction to His Philosophy, Theology and Spirituality.* New York: Harper & Brothers, 1937.

Gabriel of St. Mary Magdalen, O.C.D. *St. John of the Cross: Doctor of Divine Love and Contemplation.* Translated by a Benedictine of Stanbrook Abbey. 2nd ed. Cork: Mercier Press, 1947.

——————. *The Spiritual Director According to the Principles of St. John of the Cross.* Translated by a Benedictine of Stanbrook Abbey. Cork: Mercier Press, 1952.

Hoffman, Dominic M., O.P. *The Life Within: The Prayer of Union.* New York: Sheed and Ward, 1965.

Hughes, Catherine, ed. *Darkness and Light: Selections of St. John of the Cross.* Mysticism and Modern Man Series, Vol. I. New York: Sheed and Ward, 1972.

John of the Cross, St. *The Complete Works of Saint John of the Cross.* 3 vols. Translated and edited by E. Allison Peers from the critical edition of P. Silverio de Santa Teresa, C.D. Westminster, Md.: Newman Press, 1953.

——————. *The Collected Works of St. John of the Cross.* Translated by Kieran Kavanaugh, O.C.D. and Otilio Rodriguez, O.C.D. with introductions by Kieran Kavanaugh, O.C.D. Washington, D.C.: ICS Publications, 1973.

_____. *The Poems of St. John of the Cross*. Original Spanish texts and English versions newly revised and rewritten by John Frederick Nims. With an essay, *A Lo Divino,* by Robert Graves. New York: Grove Press, Inc., 1968.

_____. *The Mystical Doctrine of St. John of the Cross*. An abridgement made by C. H. with an introduction by R. H. J. Steuart, S.J. London: Sheed and Ward, 1944.

Johnston, William, S.J. *The Mysticism of the Cloud of Unknowing: A Modern Interpretation*. With a foreword by Thomas Merton. New York: Desclee Company, 1967.

Kranz, Gisbert. "John of the Cross," *The Modern Christian Literature*. Translated from the French by J. R. Foster. New York: Hawthorne Books, Publishers, 1961, 32-36.

Lucas de San Jose, O.C.D. *The Secret of Sanctity of St. John of the Cross*. Revised and translated by Sister Mary Albert. Milwaukee: Bruce Publishing Company, 1962.

McCann, Leonard A., C.S.B. *The Doctrine of the Void*. Toronto, Canada: The Basilian Press, n.d.

Maritain, Jacques. *The Degrees of Knowledge*. Newly translated from the fourth French edition under the supervision of Gerald B. Phelan. New York: Charles Scribner's Sons, 1959, 247-383.

Martindale, C. C., S.J. *Upon God's Holy Hill*. London: R. & T. Washbourne, Ltd., 1919, 89-152.

Medieval Mystical Tradition and St. John of the Cross. By a Benedictine of Stanbrook Abbey. Westminster, Md.: Newman Press, 1954.

Merton, Thomas. *The Ascent to Truth*. New York: Harcourt, Brace & Company, 1951.

_____. *Disputed Questions*. New York: Farrar, Straus and Cudahy, 1960, 208-217.

Peers, E. Allison. *St. John of the Cross, and other Lectures and Addresses*. 1920-1945. London: Faber & Faber, Ltd., 1956.

_____. *Spirit of Flame: A Study of St. John of the Cross*. New York: Morehouse-Gorham Co., 1945.

Simmons, Rev. Ernest. *The Fathers and Doctors of the Church*. Milwaukee: Bruce Publishing Company, 1959, 148-155.

Stein, Edith. *The Science of the Cross: A Study of St. John of the Cross*. Edited by Dr. L. Belber and Fr. Romaeus Leuven, O.C.D. Translated by Hilda Graef. Chicago: Henry Regnery Company, 1960.

ARTICLES

Bendick, J. "God and the World in John of the Cross," *Philosophy Today*, XVI (Winter, 1972), 281-294.

Culligan, Father Kevin, O.C.D. "William James and *The Varieties of*

Experience: The Birthday of a Classic," *Spiritual Life* XVIII, 1 (Spring, 1972), 15-23.

Ferraro, John. "Sanjuanist Doctrine on the Human Mode of Operation of the Theological Virtue of Faith," *Ephemerides Carmeliticae,* (1971), 250-294.

Kavanaugh, Kieran, O.C.D. "Death of God and John of the Cross," *Spiritual Life,* XII, 4 (Winter, 1966), 260-269.

_____. "Hope and Change," *Spiritual Life,* XIV, 3 (Fall, 1968), 152-165.

_____. "St. John of the Cross: On Aridity and Contemplation," *Spiritual Life,* VIII, 3 (Fall, 1962), 182-193.

_____. "St. John of the Cross: On Faith," *Spiritual Life,* V, 4 (December, 1959), 277-287.

"Mysticism of St. John," *Triumph,* VII (May, 1972), 32.

Vries, Father Piet Penning de, S.J. "All or Nothing: Carmelite Spirituality against an Ignatian Background," translated by Mrs. W. Dudok van Heel from the Dutch, *Spiritual Life,* XVII, 1 (Spring, 1971), 59-79.

Mysticism

BOOKS

An Anthology of Mysticism. Edited with an introduction and biographical notes by Paul de Jaegher, S.J. and translated by Donald Attwater and others. Westminster, Md.: Newman Press, 1950.

Augustine, St. *The Confessions of St. Augustine.* Translated with an Introduction and Notes, by John K. Ryan. Garden City, New York: Image Books, Doubleday & Company, Inc., 1960.

Baumgardt, David. *Great Western Mystics: Their Lasting Significance.* New York: Columbia University Press, 1961.

Blake, William. *The Clouded Hills: Selections.* Mysticism and Modern Man Series. Edited by Catherine Hughes. New York: Sheed and Ward, 1973.

Bridges, Hal. *American Mysticism: From William James to Zen.* New York: Harper, 1970.

Butler, Dom Cuthbert. *Western Mysticism: The Teaching of SS. Augustine, Gregory, and Bernard on Contemplation and the Contemplative Life.* New York: E. P. Dutton & Company, 1923.

Danielou, Jean. *God and the Ways of Knowing.* New York: Meridian Books, 1957.

Ebon, Martin. *Prophecy in Our Time.* New York: New American Library, 1968.

Francis de Sales, St. *The Love of God: A Treatise.* Translated and introduced by Vincent Kerns. Westminster, Maryland: The Newman Press, 1962.

Fremantle, Anne. *The Protestant Mystics.* New York: New American Library, 1965.

Graef, Hilda. *Mystics of Our Times.* Garden City, New York: Hanover House, 1962.

——————. *The Story of Mysticism.* Garden City, New York: Doubleday & Co., Inc., 1965.

——————. *The Way of Mystics.* Westminster, Md.: The Newman Bookshop, 1947.

Happold, Frederick Crossfield. *Mysticism: A Study and an Anthology.* Baltimore: Penguin Books, 1963.

Harkness, Georgia Elma. *Mysticism: Its Meaning and Message.* Nashville: Abingdon Press, 1973.

Hughes, Catherine, ed. *Dreams and Regrets: Selections from Russian Mystics.* Mysticism and Modern Man Series. New York: Sheed and Ward, 1973.

James, William. *The Varieties of Religious Experience.* Foreword by Jacques Barzun. New York: The New American Library, 1958.

Johnston, William. *Silent Music: The Science of Meditation.* Evanston: Harper & Row, Publishers, 1975.

Journet, Charles. *The Dark Knowledge of God.* Translated from the French by James F. Anderson. London: Sheed and Ward, 1948.

Knowles, David. *The Nature of Mysticism.* New York: Hawthorne Books, 1966.

McCann, J. ed. *Cloud of Unknowing.* Rev. ed. London: Burns and Oates, 1952.

Needleman, Jacob. *The New Religions.* Garden City, New York: Doubleday & Company, Inc., 1970.

——————. A. K. Bierman, James A. Gould. *Religion for a New Generation.* New York: The Macmillan Company, 1973.

Norberg, Robert B. *The Teenager and the New Mysticism. New York: Richards Rosen Press, 1973.*

O'Brien, S.J. *Varieties of Mystic Experience.* Chicago: Holt, Rinehart and Winston, 1964.

Parente, Pascal P. *The Mystical Life.* St. Louis: B. Herder Book Co., 1947.

Poulain, Aug., S.J. *The Graces of Interior Prayer: A Treatise on Mystical Theology.* Translated from the 6th ed. by Leonora L. Yorks Smith with a preface by the Rev. D. Considine, S.J. St. Louis: B. Herder, 1951.

Reinhold, H. A. ed. *The Soul Afire: Revelations of the Mystics.* Dedicated to Jacques Maritain. Pantheon Books, 1944.

Scharfstein, Ben-Ami. *Mystical Experience.* Oxford: Basil Blackwell, 1973.

Underhill, Evelyn. *Essentials of Mysticism and Other Essays*. E. P. Dutton & Co., Inc., 1960.

_____. *Mysticism: A Study in the Nature and Development of Man's Spiritual Consciousness*. Rev. ed. London: Mathuen & Co. Ltd., 1962.

_____. *The Mystics of the Church*. New York: George H. Doran Company, n.d.

_____. *The Mystic Way: A Psychological Study in Christian Origins*. New York: E. P. Dutton & Company, Inc., 1913.

_____. *Practical Mysticism: A Little Book for Normal People*. New York: E. P. Dutton & Company, 1915.

Watts, A. *Behold the Spirit: A Study in the Necessity of Mystical Religion*. New ed. New York: Pantheon Books, 1971.

White, John, ed. *What Is Meditation?* Garden City, N.Y.: Anchor Press, Doubleday, 1974.

Whitson, Robley Edward. *Mysticism and Ecumenism*. New York: Sheed and Ward, 1966.

Zaehner, R. C. *Zen, Drugs and Mysticism*. New York: Pantheon House, 1972.

ARTICLES

Alcott, E. "What is Christian Mysticism?" *Cross and Crown*, XXVI, 4 (December, 1974), 393-403.

Armstrong, A. "Christian Mysticism in the Classroom?" *Proceedings of the College Theology Society*, (1970), 287-300.

Azkout, Michael. "The Prayer of the Heart," *Review for Religious, XXXII, 1* (January, 1973), 46-50.

Bradley, Ritamary. "Present-Day Themes in the Fourteenth-Century English Mystics," *Spiritual Life* XX, 4 (Winter, 1974), 260-267.

Egan, Keith J., O. Carm. "Mysticism, Mystical Theology, and American Culture," (unpublished manuscript of Fr. Egan, Assistant Professor of Historical Theology and Spirituality, Theology Department, Marquette University, Summer, 1975).

_____. "The Prospects of the Contemporary Mystical Movement: A Critique of Mystical Theology," *Review for Religious*, XXXIV, 6 (November, 1975), 901-910.

Emery, Kent. "Translating the Mystics," *Triumph*, XI, 4 (April, 1974), 16-19.

Fitzer, Joseph. "Liturgy, Language, and Mysticism," *Worship*, XLVII, 2 (February, 1973), 66-79.

Hardy, Richard P. "Christian Mysticism: Some Ecclesial Dimensions," *Spiritual Life*, XX, 4 (Winter, 1974), 251-259.

Johnston, W. "Mystical Prayer: Can It Be Taught?" *Review for Religious*, XXVIII (September, 1969), 760-765.

_____. "Mysticism and Modern Man," *Tablet*, CCXXIII (May 24, 1969), 515.

Lamb-Novak, K. "Art and Mysticism Are a Journey," *New Catholic World*, CCXIV (May, 1973), 114-120.

Macarius, Catherine. "La Verna and Carmel: In Christian Mystical Tradition," *Spiritual Life*, XIX, 2 (Summer, 1973), 114-122.

Martin, Father, O.C.D. "Why Mysticism?" *Spiritual Life*, V, 1 (March, 1959), 22-27.

Watkin, E. I. "Mysticism," *Spiritual Life*, V, 1´ (March, 1959), 6-21.

The Occult and Drugs

BOOKS

Barber, Theodore X. *LSD, Marijuana, Yoga, and Hypnosis*. Chicago: Aldine Publishing Co., 1970.

Brenner, Joseph H. *et al*. *Drugs and Youth: Medical, Psychiatric, and Legal Facts*. New York: Liveright, 1970.

Geller, Allen and Maxwell Boas. *The Drug Beat*. New York: Cowles Book Co., 1969.

Hansen, Chadwick. *Witchcraft at Salem*. New York: New American Library, 1970.

Lennard, Henry L. and Leon J. Epstein, Arnold Bernstein, Donald C. Ransom. *Mystification and Drug Misuse: Hazards in Using Psychoactive Drugs*. San Francisco: Jossey-Bass Inc., Publishers, 1971.

Milbauer, Barbara. *Drug Abuse and Addiction: A Fact Book for Parents, Teen-Agers, and Young Adults*. New York: Crown Publishers, 1970.

Rudwin, Maximilian. *The Devil in Legend and Literature*. New York: AMS Press, 1970.

Schmidt, Philip, S.J. *Superstition and Magic*. Translated by Marie Herrerman and Rev. A. J. Peeter. Westminster, Md.: The Newman Press, 1963.

ARTICLES

Alberic, M. "My Life on Drugs—and the Grace That Saved Me," *Immaculata*, XXV, 9 (February, 1975), 6-10.

Arnett, Peter. "Disenchanted Young People Throw Off the Occult Life," *Chicago Sun-Times*, Thursday, December 25, 1975, 54.

Campbell, Robert. "The Chemistry of Madness," *Life*, (November 26, 1971), 67-68.

Fearon, J. D. "Superstition," *New Catholic Encyclopedia*, 1967, XIII, 817-818.

Kavanaugh, Kieran, O.C.D. "L.S.D. and Religious Experience II: A Theologian's Viewpoint," *Spiritual Life*, XIII, 1 (Spring, 1967), 54-63.

Kellner, Mrs. Ned. "Marijuana and Youth—Telling It as It Is," *Immaculata*, XXV, 9 (February, 1975), 4-5.

Kessler, Gary E. "The Occult Today: Why?" *Intellect*, CIV, 2369 (November, 1975), 171-174.

Meyer, Charles R. "Speak of the Devil," *Chicago Studies,* XIV, 1 (Spring, 1975), 7-18.

Navone, John. "Possession and Exorcism," *The Way,* XV, 3 (July, 1975), 163-173.

O'Leary, Brian. "Good and Evil Spirits," *The Way,* XV, 3 (July, 1975), 174-182.

Sacred Congregation for the Doctrine of the Faith. "Christian Faith and Demonology," *The Pope Speaks,* XX, 3 and 4 (Winter, 1975), 209-238.

> A study recommended as a sure basis for grasping the teaching of the magisterium on Faith and Demonology.

Tapia, Ralph J. "Psychedelics, Mysticism and Morality," *Thought,* XLV, 177 (Summer, 1970), 235-352.

Movements from the East

BOOKS

Dechanet, J. M., O.S.B. *Christian Yoga.* New York: Harper & Brothers Publishers, 1960.

Eliade, Mircea. Yoga: *Immortality and Freedom.* Princeton, N.J.: Princeton University Press, 1970.

Fuerstein, George and Jeanine Miller. *Yoga and Beyond: Essays in Indian Philosophy.* New York: Schocken, 1972.

Graham, Aelred. *Zen Catholicism.* New York: Harcourt, Brace, and World, 1963.

Harper, Marvin H. *Gurus, Swami, and Avators: Spiritual Masters and Their American Disciples.* Philadelphia: Westminster, 1972.

Hassan, Mohain A. "The Hare Krishna Movement," a thesis presented to the Graduate School of Sociology at De Paul University, May, 1972.

Johnston, William. *The Still Point: Reflections on Zen and Christian Mysticism.* New York: Harper and Row Publishers, 1971.

Jung, C. G. *Psychology and Religion:* West and East. Translated by R. F. C. Hull. Bollingen Series XX. New York: Pantheon Books, Inc., 1958.

Merton, Thomas. *Mystics and Zen Masters.* New York: Farrar, Strauss and Giroux, 1967.

Mishra, Rammurti. *Fundamentals of Yoga.* New York: Lancer, 1969.

_____. *The Textbook of Yoga Psychology.* New York: Julian Press, 1963.

Staal, J. F. and A. C. Bhaktivedanta Swami. *The Krishna Consciousness Movement Is the Genuine Vedic Way.* Boston: ISKCON Press, 1970.

Suzuki, Shunryu. *Zen Mind, Beginner's Mind.* New York: Walker/Weatherhill, 1970.

Watts, Alan W. *Psychotherapy East and West*. New York: Mentor Books, 1961.

Wood, Ernest. *Yoga*. Baltimore: Penguin Books, 1973.

ARTICLES

Campbell, Thomas L., C.S.C. "Prayer in the Eastern Religions," *Sisters Today,* XLV, 4 (December, 1973), 207-211.

Fackre, G. "Going East: Neomysticism and Christian Faith," *Christian Century,* LXXXVIII (April 14, 1971), 457-461.

Gintoft, Ethel. "Yoga Influencing U.S. Youth Called 'Phony,' " *The Catholic Herald Citizen,* vol. 104, n. 3, December 1, 1973, pp. 1 and 10.

Grassi, Joseph A. "Christian Mantras: The Rediscovering and Power of an Ancient Approach to Inner Christian Transformation," *Worship,* XLIX, 9 (November, 1975), 530-542.

Haglof, Anthony, O.C.D. "Psychology, Contemplation and the East," *Spiritual Life,* XVIII, 3 (Fall, 1972), 154-165.

Hamelin, Sister Marie, R.J.M. "Yoga—Yes or No?" *Review for Religious,* XXX, 4 (July, 1974), 817-827.

Johnston, William, S.J. "Zen and Christian Contemplation," *Review for Religious,* XXIX (September, 1970), 699-704.

Maloney, George A., S.J. "Christian Yoga and Contemplation," *Review for Religious,* XXXI, 3 (May, 1972), 411-418.

Mangini, Father Richard A., "Hinduism Is Not Christianity," *The Catholic Herald Citizen,* January 10, 1976, p. 8.

Mano, D. K. "Krishna Kids," *National Review,* XXV (February 16, 1973.)

Meyers, H. E. "Yoga," *New Catholic Encyclopedia,* 1967, XIV, 1071-1073.

Panikkar, R. "The Ultimate Experience," *Theological Digest,* (Autumn, 1972), 219-226.

Paul VI, Pope. "The Christian Is an Apostle," *The Pope Speaks,* XX, 3 and 4 (Winter, 1975), 196-198.

Peano, Maria, O.C.D. "Eastern Prayer—Yoga," *Spiritual Life,* XVIII, 3 (Fall, 1972), 174-186.

Rowe, Sister Margaret. "Current Trends in Prayer," *Spiritual Life,* XVII, 3 (Fall, 1971), 172-185.

——————————. "The Fire and the Rose," *Spiritual Life,* XVIII, 3 (Fall, 1972), 187-197.

Sullivan, Father Lawrence, O.C.D. "Lao Tzu and the Doctrine of the Way," *Spiritual Life,* XVIII, 3 (Fall, 1972), 166-173.

The Present Christian Movements

BOOKS

Ellwood, Jr., Robert S. *One Way: The Jesus Movement and Its Meaning*. Englewood Cliffs, New Jersey: Prentice-Hall, Inc., 1973.

Ford, Clay. *Berkeley Journal: Jesus and the Street People*. New York: Harper and Row, 1972.

Graham, Billy. *The Jesus Generation*. Grand Rapids, Mich.: Zenderman Publishing House, 1971.

O'Connor, Edward D., C.S.C. *The Pentecostal Movement*. Notre Dame, Indiana: Ave Maria Press, 1971.

——————. *Pentecost in the Modern World*. Notre Dame, Indiana: Ave Maria Press, 1972.

Plowman, Edward E. *The Jesus Movement in America* (formerly called "The Underground Church"): *Accounts of Christian Revolutionaries in Action*. Elgin, Ill.: David C. Cook Publishing Co., 1971.

Streiker, Lowell D. *The Jesus Trip: Advent of the Jesus Freaks*. Abingdon Press, 1972.

ARTICLES

Blouin, Brother Francis. "Religious and the Charismatic Movement," *Review for Religious,* XXXIV, 1 (January, 1975), 71-77.

"Charismatic Renewal: A Message of the Canadian Bishops," *Catholic Mind,* LXXIV, 1296 (October, 1975), 55-64.

Del Monte Sol, Teresa. "Pentecostalism and the Doctrine of Saint Teresa and Saint John of the Cross," *Spiritual Life,* XVII, 1 (Spring, 1971), 21-33.

Donohue, John W. "High on Jesus," *America,* CXXIX, 3 (August 4, 1973), 66-67.

Ford J. Massingberd. "American Catholic Neo-Pentecostalism," *Catholic Mind,* LXXIV, 1299 (January, 1976), 43-52.

——————. "Fly United—But Not in Too Close Formation: Reflections on the Catholic Pentecostal Movement," *Spiritual Life,* XVII, 1 (Spring, 1971), 12-20.

——————. "Pentecostal Poise or Docetic Charismatics?" *Spiritual Life,* XIX, 1 (Spring, 1973), 32-47.

——————. "Tongues—Leadership—Women: Further Reflections on the Neo-Pentecostal Movement," *Spiritual Life,* XVII, 3 (Fall, 1971), 186-197.

Futrell, John Carroll, S.J. "Charismatic Renewal in Historical Perspective," *Review for Religious,* XXIV, 1 (January, 1975), 78-79.

Haglof, Anthony, O.C.D. "On Spirit-Baptism and Religious Commitment," manuscript, Peterborough, New Hampshire, June, 1974.

——————. "Psychology and the Pentecostal Experience," *Spiritual Life,* XVII, 3 (Fall, 1971), 198-210.

Jorstad, Erling T. "From Drugs to Jesus," *Catholic Mind,* LXX (December, 1972), 14-21.

Kelsey, Morton T. "Speaking in Tongues in 1971: An Assessment of Its Meaning and Value," *Review for Religious,* XXX, 2 (March, 1971), 245-255.

McDonnell, Kilian. "A Sociologist Looks at the Catholic Charismatic Renewal," *Worship,* XLIX, 7 (August-September, 1975), 378-392.

Murphy, Father Lawrence. "The Jesus Movement: A Critique," *Catholic Mind,* LXXI (March, 1973), 4-6.

Nauer, Barbara. "The Intellectual and the Charismatic," *America* (July 27, 1972), 26-29.

"The New Rebel Cry: Jesus Is Coming," *Time,* (June 21, 1971), 58-63.

Osowski, Fabian, O.C.S.O. "Pentecost and Pentecostals," *Review for Religious,* XXVII, 6 (November, 1968), 1064-1088.

Extensive Bibliography.

Paul VI, Pope. "The Holy Spirit and the Blessed Virgin," *The Pope Speaks,* XX, 2 (Fall, 1975), 101-106.

Letter to Cardinal Leo Jozef Suenens prior to the coming of the International Marian Congress.

_____. "The New Life of Pentecost," *The Pope Speaks,* XX, 2 (Fall, 1975), 107-111.

Feast day homily encouraging Christians to abandon themselves to the Holy Spirit.

_____. "Principles of Spiritual Discernment," *The Pope Speaks,* XX, 2 (Fall, 1975), 175-179.

Address to the Third International Congress of the Catholic Charismatic Movement.

"Vatican Weekly Defends Charismatic Movement," *The New World,* December 26, 1975, p. 1.

Contemporary Spirituality

BOOKS

Balthasar, Hans Urs von. *Prayer.* Translated by A. V. Littledale, New York: Sheed and Ward, 1961.

Basset, Bernard, S.J. *Let's Start Praying Again: Field Work in Meditation.* New York: Herder and Herder, 1972.

Bloom, Archbishop Anthony. *Beginning to Pray.* New York: Paulist Press, 1970.

_____. *God and Man.* New York: The Newman Press, 1971.

_____. *Living Prayer.* Springfield: Templegate Publishers, 1966.

"An Orthodox prelate" shares with us "the rich resources of the Eastern heritage of prayer...by presenting with pastoral simplicity and priestly concern the place of prayer in the daily concerns of modern Christians." John Wright, Bishop of Pittsburg.

Bouyer, Louis, Cong. Orat. *Introduction to Spirituality.* Translated by Mary Perkins Ryan. Collegeville: Liturgical Press, 1961.

Dubay, Thomas, S.M. *God Dwells Within Us.* Denville, New Jersey: Dimension Books, 1971.

_____. *Pilgrims Pray.* New York: Alba House, 1974.

Egan, Keith J., O. Carm. *What Is Prayer?* Denville, N.J.: Dimension Books, 1973.

Farrell, Edward, S.T.L. *Prayer Is a Hunger.* Denville, N.J.: Dimension Books, 1972.

Galli, Mario von, S.J. *Living Our Future: Francis of Assisi and the Church of Tomorrow.* Translated by Maureen Sullivan and John Drury, with color photos by Dennis Stock. Chicago: Franciscan Herald Press, 1972.

Gleason, Robert W., S.J. *The Indwelling Spirit.* Staten Island, N.Y.: Alba House, 1966.

Goichon, A.M. *Contemplative Life in the World.* Translated by M. A. Bouchard. St. Louis, Mo.: B. Herder Book Co., 1958.

Graef, Hilda C. *God in Our Daily Life.* Westminster, Md.: The Newman Press, 1951.

Guillerand, Dom Augustin, O.Cart. *The Prayer of the Presence of God.* Translated from the French by a Monk of Parkminster. Wilkes-Barre, Penn.: Dimension books, 1966.

Happold, F. C. *Religious Faith and the Twentieth-Century Man.* Baltimore: Penguin Books, 1966.

Hinnebusch, Paul, O.P. *Prayer, the Search for Authenticity.* New York: Sheed and Ward, 1969.

_____. *Dynamic Contemplation.* New York: Sheed and Ward, 1970.

Kreyche, Robert J. *The Making of a Saint: A Guide to the Spiritual Life.* New York: Alba House, 1973.

Leclercq, Jacques, Canon. *The Interior Life.* Translated from the French by Fergus Murphy. New York: P. J. Kenedy & Sons, 1961.

Lekeux, Martial, O.F.M. *The Art of Prayer.* Translated by Paul Joseph Oligny, O.F.M. Chicago: Franciscan Herald Press, 1959.

Lotz, Johannes B. *Interior Prayer: The Exercise of Personality.* Translated by Dominic B. Gerlach, C.PP.S. New York: Herder and Herder, 1969.

Maritain, Jacques. *Approaches to God.* Translated from the French by Peter O'Reilly. New York: The Macmillan Co., 1965.

Merton, Thomas. *Contemplative Prayer.* New York: Herder and Herder, 1969.

_____. *New Seeds of Contemplation.* Norfolk, Conn.: New Direction.

_____. *Contemplation in a World of Action.* Introduction by Jean Leclercq, O.S.B. Garden City, N.Y.: Doubleday & Company, Inc., 1971.

Mooney, Christopher F., S.J. ed. *Prayer: The Problem of Dialogue With God.* Papers of the 1968 Bea Institute Symposium. New York: Paulist Press, 1969.

Nouwen, Henri J. M. *Pray to Live: Thomas Merton: A Contemplative Critic.* Translated by David Schlaver, C.S.C. Notre Dame: Ave Maria Press, 1972.

_____. *With Open Hands*. Photography by Ron P. van den Bosch and Theo Robert. Notre Dame: Ave Maria Press, 1972.

hilipon, M. M., O.P. *The Spiritual Doctrine of Sister Elizabeth of the Trinity*. Translated by a Benedictine of Stanbrook Abbey. Westminster, Md.: The Newman Bookshop, 1947.

Pieper, Josef. *Happiness and Contemplation*. Translated by Richard and Clara Winston. New York: Pantheon Books Inc., 1958.

_____. *Leisure the Basis of Culture*. New York: The New American Library, 1963.

Plus, Raoul, S.J. *In Christ Jesus*. Revised and Corrected Edition. Translated by Peter Addison. London: Burns Oates and Washbourne, Ltd., 1948.

_____.*The Path to the Heights*. Westminster, Maryland: The Newman Press, 1954.

Savary, Louis M. and Thomas J. O'Connor, comp. *Finding God*. New York: Newman Press, 1971.

Thibaut, Dom Raymond. *Union With God*. According to the letters of Direction of Dom Marmion. Introductory letter of Archbishop Goodier, S.J. Translated from the French by Mother Mary Saint Thomas. London: Sands & Co., 1960.

Turro, James. *Reflections: Path to Prayer*. Chicago: R. R. Donnelly & Sons Co., 1972.

Vatican II. *Dogmatic Constitution on the Church*. Boston: St. Paul Editions, 1967.

Vawter, Bruce. *This Man Jesus: An Essay Toward a New Testament Christology*. Garden City, New York: Doubleday & Company, Inc. 1973.

Von Hildebrand, Dietrich. *The Art of Living*. Chicago: Franciscan Herald Press, 1965.

_____. *Transformation in Christ*. New York: Longmans, Green and Co., 1948.

Yzermans, Vincent A., *American Participation in the Second Vatican Council*. New York: Sheed and Ward, 1967.

ARTICLES

Beha, Marie, O.S.C. "The Leisure to be Contemplative," *Spiritual Life*, XX, 4 (Winter, 1974), 238-247.

Borst, J., M.H.M. "A Method of Contemplative Prayer," *Review for Religious*, XXX, 4 (July, 1974), 790-816.

College, Edmund, O.S.A. "When You Pray: The Prayer of Imitation," *The Way*, XIII, 1 (January, 1973), 67-76.
         First of the series on prayer.

Condon, Helen, R.S.C.J. "The Prayer Question," *Review for Religious*, XXXI, 6 (November, 1972), 901-914.

Deeken, Alfons, S.J. "A Trinitarian Spirituality for Today," *Review for Religious*, XXXI, 2 (March, 1972), 237-246.

Dubay, Thomas, S.M. "Classical Spirituality: Contemporary?" *Review for Religious*, XXIII, (July, 1964), 445-466.

_____. "Indwelling: Transfiguring Consummation," *Review for Religious.* XXVII, 2 (March, 1968), 223-242.

Eliseus, Father, O.C.D. "Contemplation Is for All," *Spiritual Life,* IX, 4 (Winter, 1963), 267-275.

Finley, James J. "The Silent Search for God: Trappists of Gethsemani," *Our Sunday Visitor,* October 14, 1973, pp. 1, 8 and 9.

Flavin, Genevieve. "A Habit of Love Prevails Behind These Doors," *Chicago Tribune,* sec. 2, May 24, 1973, p. 21.

Garascia, Sister Mary, C.PP.S. "Prayer and Spirituality," *Review for Religious,* XXXI, 6 (November, 1972), 915-920.

Gramlich, Sister Miriam Louise, I.H.M. "Contemplation and Creativity," *Cross and Crown,* XXVII, 1 (March, 1975), 25-34.

_____. "A 'Future Shock' Absorber," *Spiritual Life,* XVIII, 3 (Fall, 1972), 147-153.

Hanlon, Morgan, C.P. "The Spirituality of Thomas Merton," *Sisters Today,* (December, 1972), 198-210.

Houle, Sister Marie Agnes, SSJ. "Towards Tomorrow's Task: Contemplation," *Sisters Today,* XLII, 6 (February, 1971), 300-306.

John Casimir, Father, O.C.D. "Edith Stein and the Modern Woman," *Spiritual Life,* VIII, 2 (Summer, 1962), 127-131.

Kiesling, Christopher, O.P. "Faith in a Time of Confusion," *Cross and Crown,* XXIII, 1 (March, 1971), 53-61.

Kilduff, Thomas, O.C.D. "Work, Leisure and Contemplation," *Spiritual Life,* XVI, 3 (Fall, 1970), 183-201.

_____. "A New Form of Austerity for the Contemporary World," *Spiritual Life,* XIII, 1 (Spring, 1967), 29-37.

Latimer, Christopher, O.C.D. "A Love for People," *Spiritual Life,* XVI, 1 (Spring, 1970), 42-49.

Leclercq, Jean, Pere, O.S.B. "Is There Such a Thing as Contemplative Prayer?" *Spiritual Life,* XVII, 1 (Spring, 1971), 34-39.

_____. "New Forms of Contemplation and of the Contemplative Life," *Theological Studies,* (1972), 307-319.

Macarius, Catherine. "Prayer in Perspective," *Way: Catholic Viewpoints,* XXIX, 1 (January-February, 1973), 34-41.
First of a series on contemplation for the laity.

_____. "Intuition and Conversion," *Way: Catholic Viewpoints,* XXIX, 2 (March, 1973), 24-31.

_____. "Bandwagon," *Way: Catholic Viewpoints,* XXIX, 3 (April, 1973), 2-10.

_____. "Metanoia: Prayer and Discipline," *Way: Catholic Viewpoints,* XXIX, 4 (May, 1973), 25-31.

_____. "A Technique for Prayer?" *Way: Catholic Viewpoints,* XXIX, 5 (June, 1973), 4-11.

_____. "Prayer and Poverty," *Way: Catholic Viewpoints,* XXIX, 7 (September, 1973), 18-27.

McBennett, Sister M. Annette, R.S.M. "Spiritual Reading," *Sisters Today*, XLV, 4 (December, 1973), 212-220.

Maeder, Michael, O.S.B. "Being Human: A Study of Friedrich von Hugel." *Sisters Today*, (December, 1972), 183-196.

Maloney, Geo. A., S.J. "The Jesus Prayer: The Prayer of Modern Man," *Spiritual Life*, XVI, 2 (Summer, 1970), 102-108.

Meissner, W. W., S.J. "Notes on the Psychology of Hope," *Journal of Religion and Health*, (1973), 120-139.

Merton, Thomas. "Prayer, Tradition and Experience," Ed. by Naomi Burton Stone, *Sisters Today*, XLII, 6 (February, 1971), 285-293.

Michael of the Holy Family, O.C.D. "The Normalcy of Contemplation," *Spiritual Life*, II, 4 (December, 1956), 245-253.

Morgan, John H. "The Secret of the Desert," *Cross and Crown*, XXVII, 2 (June, 1975), 148-155.

Morry, Matthew F., O.P. "Mary and the Contemporary Scene," *Marian Studies*, (1972), 133-153.

Muto, Susan Annette. "Solitude, Self-Presence and True Participation," *Spiritual Life*, XX, 4 (Winter, 1974), 231-237.

O'Donovan, Daniel, O.C.R. "Prayer Today," *Sursum Corda*, (1972), 241-248.

Ottenstroer, Sister Joann, P.B.V.M. "Functional Approach to Silence," *Review for Religious*, XXVII, 2 (March, 1968), 208-222.

Paul VI, Pope. "Address on Spirituality," *L'Osservatore Romano*, English edition, n. 10 (258), March 8, 1973, p. 1.

_____. "Renewal of Devotion to Mary," *The Pope Speaks*, XX, 3 and 4 (Winter, 1975), 199-203.
    Address to the International Mariological and Marian Congress.

Quinn, Gary J. "On Christian Life in the Future: The Need for Contemplation," *Chicago Studies*, XIII, 1 (Spring, 1974), 77-87.

Regan, George M., C.M. "Spirituality in a Time of Transition," *Review for Religious*, XXXII, 5 (September, 1973), 989-1001.

Riga, Peter J. "Demands of Love," *Spiritual Life*, XVI, 1 (Spring, 1970), 4-18.

Rigali, Norbert. "Faith, Hope and Love," *Chicago Studies*, XIII, 3 (Fall, 1974), 253-264.

Ruthmann, Sister Marie Therese, V.M.H. "Celebrating Leisure Today," *Review for Religious*, XXXII, 3 (May, 1973), 541-556.

Schoeler, Sisters Marjorie and Mary Thaddeus Thom, O.S.F. "Contemplation and Solitude in Franciscan Life," *The Cord*, XXIV, 8 (September, 1974), 280-289 and 9 (October, 1974), 317-327.

Scott, Sister M. Valeria. "Women and Prayer," *Spirit and Life*, LXIV, 8 (January, 1969), 20-27.

"Search for Faith," *Life*, LXVIII (January 9, 1970), 16-26.

Sheets, J. R. "Personal and Liturgical Prayer," *Worship*, XLVII, 7 (August-September, 1973), 415-416.

Smith, Herbert F. "Contemplation: Option or Human Imperative," *Homiletic and Pastoral Review*, LXXIII, 8 (May, 1973), 17-24.

_____. "A Contemplative in Action a Multiple View," *Cross and Crown*, XXVI, 3 (September, 1974), 280-295.

Steere, Douglas V. "The Spirituality of Friedrich von Hugel," *Worship*, XLVII, 9 (November, 1973), 540-546.

Stein, Waultraul J. "Edith Stein, Twenty-five Years Later," *Spiritual Life*, XIII, 4 (Winter, 1967), 244-251.

Thomas, F. G. "The Need for Prayer," *Life and Worship*, (October, 1972), 19-23.

Voillaume, Father Rene. "Contemplation in the Church in Our Time," *Spiritual Life*, XVII, 1 (Spring, 1971), 40-58.

Watkin, E. I. "Contemplation and Worship," *Spiritual Life*, XVI, 2 (Summer, 1970), 109-116.

Daughters of St. Paul

IN MASSACHUSETTS
50 St. Paul's Ave., Jamaica Plain, Boston, MA 02130;
617-522-8911; 617-522-0875.
172 Tremont Street, Boston, MA 02111; **617-426-5464;**
617-426-4230.

IN NEW YORK
78 Fort Place, Staten Island, NY 10301; **212-447-5071; 212-447-5086.**
59 East 43rd Street, New York, NY 10017; **212-986-7580.**
625 East 187th Street, Bronx, NY 10458; **212-584-0440.**
525 Main Street, Buffalo, NY 14203; **716-847-6044.**

IN NEW JERSEY
Hudson Mall — Route 440 and Communipaw Ave.,
Jersey City, NJ 07304; **201-433-7740.**

IN CONNECTICUT
202 Fairfield Ave., Bridgeport, CT 06604; **203-335-9913.**

IN OHIO
2105 Ontario Street (at Prospect Ave.), Cleveland, OH 44115;
216-621-9427.
25 E. Eighth Street, Cincinnati, OH 45202; **513-721-4838;**
513-421-5733.

IN PENNSYLVANIA
1719 Chestnut Street, Philadelphia, PA 19103; **215-568-2638.**

IN VIRGINIA
1025 King Street, Alexandria, VA 22314; **703-683-1741;**
703-549-3806.

IN FLORIDA
2700 Biscayne Blvd., Miami, FL 33137; **305-573-1618.**

IN LOUISIANA
4403 Veterans Memorial Blvd., Metairie, LA 70002; **504-887-7631;**
504-887-0113.
1800 South Acadian Thruway, P.O. Box 2028, Baton Rouge, LA 70821;
504-343-4057; 504-381-9485.

IN MISSOURI
1001 Pine Street (at North 10th), St. Louis, MO 63101; **314-621-0346;**
314-231-1034.

IN ILLINOIS
172 North Michigan Ave., Chicago, IL 60601; **312-346-4228;**
312-346-3240.

IN TEXAS
114 Main Plaza, San Antonio, TX 78205; **512-224-8101.**

IN CALIFORNIA
1570 Fifth Ave., San Diego, CA 92101; **619-232-1442.**
46 Geary Street, San Francisco, CA 94108; **415-781-5180.**

IN HAWAII
1143 Bishop Street, Honolulu, HI 96813; **808-521-2731.**

IN ALASKA
750 West 5th Ave., Anchorage, AK 99501; **907-272-8183.**

IN CANADA
3022 Dufferin Street, Toronto 395, Ontario, Canada.

IN ENGLAND
128, Notting Hill Gate, London W11 3QG, England.
133 Corporation Street, Birmingham B4 6PH, England.
5A-7 Royal Exchange Square, Glasgow G1 3AH, England.
82 Bold Street, Liverpool L1 4HR, England.

IN AUSTRALIA
58 Abbotsford Rd., Homebush, N.S.W. 2140, Australia